Understanding

Special

Educational

Needs

owl

Understanding Special Educational Needs

A Teacher's Guide to Effective School-based Research

RUTH KERSHNER AND ROLAND CHAPLAIN

David Fulton Publishers
London

David Fulton Publishers Ltd
Ormond House, 26–27 Boswell Street, London WC1N 3JZ

www.fultonpublishers.co.uk

First published in Great Britain by David Fulton Publishers 2001

British Library Cataloguing in Publication Data
A catalogue record for this book is available from the British Library.

ISBN 1-85346-718-9

The publishers would like to thank Rosemary Appleyard for copy-editing and Priscilla Sharland for proofreading this book.

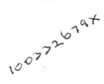

Typeset by Textype Typesetters, Cambridge
Printed in Great Britain by The Cromwell Press Ltd, Trowbridge, Wilts.

Contents

To Annick

CHAPTER 1

SEN and school-based research: why this book now?

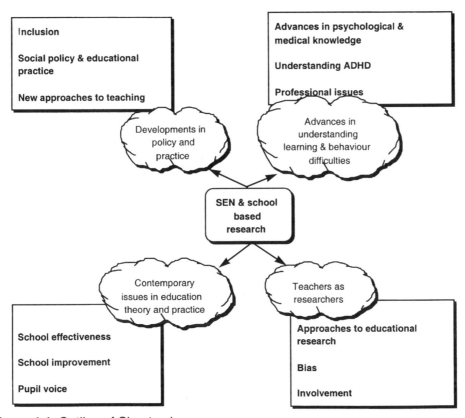

Figure 1.1 Outline of Chapter 1

In this chapter we examine four key areas which help to explain why a new book about the use of school-based research as an approach to understanding special educational needs (SEN) may be useful to teachers. These four areas (Figure 1.1) concern:

- developments in the policy and practice of teaching pupils with SEN;
- advances in the understanding of learning and behaviour difficulties;
- contemporary issues in education theory and practice – the bigger picture;
- teachers as researchers.

The following sections focus on significant changes and reinterpretations which have taken place in recent years in each of these areas. Their combined impact makes a strong case for teachers to engage in school-based research as a means of developing and expanding their professional knowledge, understanding and skills so as to help *all* pupils to learn in school, including those identified as having SEN.

Developments in the policy and practice of teaching pupils with SEN

Since the 1981 Education Act, the heated debates about 'integration' in the 1980s and 'inclusion' in the last decade have been accompanied by equally controversial pressures to identify and provide for pupils who, compared to their peers, seem to face particular and persistent difficulties in learning – examples of which include specific literacy difficulties, autism, emotional and behavioural difficulties (EBD) or attention deficit and hyperactivity disorder (ADHD).

Early writers on integration argued for an educational system in which all children had a right to attend a local mainstream school (see, for example, Dessent 1987). Although some children, it was suggested, required special attention and adaptations for their 'special' educational needs (usually practical and financial support in the form of additional staffing and/or special resources). More recently, writers such as Hart (1996) have taken a different perspective in suggesting that inclusion requires a new type of 'innovative thinking' in which the focus is upon opportunities in the learning environment rather than the special educational needs of individual children (see also, Ainscow 1999; Mittler 2000). Thus, a child may have a learning or behaviour difficulty when it is clear that he or she is expected to learn something or behave in a certain way, in certain circumstances, often within a limited time span (McDermott 1996).

Current SEN policy and practice, as represented in the 1998 Action Programme (DfEE 1998a) appear to be attempting to incorporate both approaches by seeking to develop:

- an inclusive educational system which will both improve the educational opportunities and outcomes for all children;
- a range of special educational provisions to improve educational opportunities and outcomes for children with complex needs or particular types or patterns of difficulty in learning in the ordinary school system.

These goals are often forced into competition with each other in situations where prioritisation of limited educational resources is necessary, or where professionals may have a vested interest in one particular perspective. The experience of working with individual pupils in school can highlight the difficulty in balancing the urgency of coping with pupils' immediate needs against the longer-term changes to legislation, policy and practice. Yet the two goals do not need to be in opposition. We would argue that to focus on *either* the context *or* the individual child can result in a wasteful division of effort in both teaching and research. Recent understandings of SEN bring together an interest in how individuals and groups of children learn in different contexts (see, for example, Norwich 2000; Skidmore 1999a; Clark *et al.* 1998; Hart 1996). Teachers can be involved in examining how policy and practice in a school may create or prevent SEN alongside making decisions for individual pupils in the light of the increasingly sophisticated knowledge of why certain children have persistent difficulties in learning.

The 1998 SEN Action Programme (DfEE 1998a) was pragmatic in recognising the limitations of a broad policy of inclusion which does not take individual circumstances into account. The government found in the responses to the previous Green Paper *Excellence for All Children: Meeting special educational needs* (DfEE 1997) that:

> Many, particularly practising classroom teachers, were concerned that we should not underestimate the real challenges schools face in becoming more inclusive. Our approach will be practical, not dogmatic, and will put the needs of individual children first. (p. 23)

So, what challenges do schools face and how can the needs of individual children be identified in different school contexts? These questions need investigation – the answers are not easily understood or agreed. In considering the role of school-based research in this area we need to recognise the changes taking place at different levels of the education system and the interactions between them.

There have been a number of recent developments in the field of special educational needs and 'allied' provision. Some of these developments have resulted from changes to policy, practice and attitudes towards the education and care of children with special educational needs; while others reflect advances in mainstream medical and psychological research and practice (see Table 1.1 for examples). Some changes to educational practice come in the form of central government directives to schools, (e.g. from the Department for Education and Employment (DfEE), Department of Health (DOH) and Home Office) others from initiatives which reflect more local concerns.

Social policy and educational practice – a suitable case for research?

While a number of developments and directives reflect the findings of empirical educational research, others are driven by changes to economic and social policy. A recent example of the latter comes from concerns about children's rights and equal opportunity legislation. The Children Act 1989 for example, heralded a new status for children. Subsequent guidance and further changes had significant outcomes for professionals working with children generally and, in particular, those working with the most vulnerable children. Staff working with children who exhibit challenging behaviour for example, are aware of the ongoing debate regarding restraint of those individuals perceived to be out of control and a danger to themselves or others. This debate has involved both educational and social services departments and led to the formulation of guidelines in local authorities on permissible forms of physical interventions with children and young people (see, for example, DfEE 1998b; DOH 1993; DfEE 2000a).

This concern is not limited to special educational needs, but is part of a bigger picture. We are made increasingly aware of difficulties outside education regarding what constitutes 'reasonable force' and where and when not to intervene with individuals breaking social codes with their behaviour – for example; military peace keeping, policing of demonstrations and protecting oneself from personal attack. This bigger picture reflects changes to human rights and to the execution of the law, including substantial changes to individual rights, litigation and compensation. For the teacher in a classroom these issues can appear to have little if anything to do with what they are faced with on a daily basis. However, the level of public interest and monitoring of service delivery and professional practice currently taking place in schools in the form of OFSTED, alongside accountability to parents and governors, tends to contradict such thinking.

From a research perspective, analysing the 'big picture' and relating it to a more local context can be quite illuminating. In their book, *Caring Under Pressure* (1994), Chaplain and Freeman related the very local experiences of young people in residential schools to the wider issues of welfare justice and a historical perspective. In so doing, political rhetoric and official recommendations were contrasted with the reality of practice. Furthermore, these observations were analysed within a historical frame which highlighted those areas where progress had been made and those which had marked time.

This unpacking of rhetoric from reality, especially the translation of political 'fantasy' into workable practice for professionals, is familiar rather than novel in some areas of social science. In fields such as special education, given the relatively small populations of those involved, this can sometimes appear more difficult to do. However, prospective researchers should not be put off analysing the effects of policy changes on professional practice within, and across disciplines. Researching the effects of change can prove an interesting (if often sensitive) area of study. While change can be motivating for those involved, it can also prove stressful requiring the development of new coping strategies and new ways of working.

Table 1.1 New approaches to teaching pupils with SEN

The list below contains examples of some of the more recent developments which have been well-publicised, together with a few relevant references. The list is not exhaustive.

General approaches which help all pupils to learn in school	
Developing thinking skills and learning to learn	Ashman and Conway (1997) Whitebread (2000)
Responding to pupils' individual differences, learning styles and preferences	Babbage *et al.* (1999) Gardner (1993) Kershner (2000)
Using ICT to support learning	Littleton and Light (1999) McFarlane (1997) Monteith (2000)
Listening to pupils' views	Rudduck *et al.* (1995) Davie and Galloway (1996)
Curriculum development	Robbins (2000)
Developing peer tutoring/groupwork	Kutnick and Manson (2000)
Enhancing pupils' motivation	Chaplain (2000a)
Specific teaching strategies and resources for pupils with certain types of special educational needs	
Planning and teaching for pupils with dyslexia	Tod (2000)
Supporting pupils with syndromes such as dyspraxia	Portwood (2000)
Using social stories with autistic children	Rowe (1999) Gray (1994)
Teaching and learning with 'Enabling Technology'	Blamires (1999) Bozic and Murdoch (1996)
Enhancing self-esteem and emotional development	Mosley (1996) Urquhart (2000)
School development and multidisciplinary teamwork	
Setting up teacher support teams	Creese *et al.* (1997)
Inclusion initiatives and staff development	CSIE (2000) Mittler (2000)
Developing early years multidisciplinary interventions	Wolfendale (2000)

Advances in the understanding of learning and behaviour difficulties

There have been a number of advances in psychological, medical and educational research which have the potential to change the way in which teachers (and other professionals) perceive, investigate and intervene with children who have special educational needs. These advances include, for example: cognitive functioning *vis-à-vis* the enhancement of academic achievement among children with SEN (Adey and Shayer 1994); overcoming the limitations of motor difficulties using conductive educational methods (Sigafoos *et al.* 1993); cognitive models of ADHD (Rutter 1989); cognition and achievement motivation (Galloway *et al.* 1996) and metacognition and hearing difficulties (Al-Hilawani 2000). See Table 1.1 for further examples.

However, while a number of professionals research SEN, they often come to very different conclusions about the causes of, and how to respond to, learning and behavioural difficulties. As an illustration of such differences we will examine the professional discourses in one area of SEN in more detail. In the next section we discuss some of the psychological, medical and educational research findings and debates surrounding an area which has attracted considerable interest from both professionals and lay persons, that is, attention deficit hyperactivity disorder (ADHD).

ADHD – A problem of definition?

Attention deficit hyperactivity disorder is defined by Cooper and Ideus (2000) as:

> . . . a medical diagnosis that is applied to children and adults who are experiencing significant behavioural and cognitive difficulties in important aspects of their lives (e.g. in their familial and personal relationship; at school or work). These difficulties can be attributed to problems of impulse control, hyperactivity and inattention. (p. 1)

ADHD is one of a cluster of terms relating to behaviours displayed by sufferers such as, inattention and difficulties regulating impulsiveness. As in some other areas of SEN, behaviour difficulties are difficult to define – and ADHD is no exception. Anyone familiar with the literature concerned with the definition and aetiology of maladjustment or emotional and behavioural difficulties will understand that precise definitions in this area are elusive to say the least (see Laslett 1983; Chaplain 2000b).

Attempts to explain the aetiology of ADHD are wide-ranging and often controversial as are debates about treatment, especially in respect of using medication to manage children's behaviour (see, for example, www.attention-deficit-disorder.org). The field has attracted the interest of a number of research communities including psychiatrists (e.g. Rutter 1989), psychologists (e.g. Braswell and Bloomquist 1991) and educationalists (e.g. Cooper and Ideus 2000). Explanations include social construction; mild brain damage and multi-modal perspectives.

The causes of ADHD – professional discourses

According to Tannock (1998), ADHD occurs more frequently among the biological relatives of children diagnosed as having ADHD compared with the incidence among relatives of other children. This has led some writers to argue that ADHD might somehow be inherited. In response, critics of this view argue that controlling for environmental factors which families are likely to experience or share, such as stress or poverty, is difficult. Nevertheless, investigators have acknowledged an association between a clear genetic anomaly and individuals identified as having ADHD (Hauser *et al.* 1993). Gene structures in the Dopamine system (which is concerned with regulation of the mind) appear to be important in distinguishing between individuals who have ADHD and those who do not (Thompson 1993). Beyond debates about causality are those related to treatment, particularly in relation to the use of drugs to control behaviour. The use of psychostimulants (e.g. Ritalin) to control the behaviour of children with ADHD, has sparked off a heated debate among a number of professionals and parents. These drugs have remarkable effects – usually within an hour of swallowing a single dose the child becomes more obedient, more focused and more willing to concentrate on tasks and instructions. Those having difficulty with a child can simply administer a tablet and he/she will become less trouble-some. While the appeal of using such drugs might be to offer some respite to those having to cope with the child, the side effects are considered unacceptable by many professionals. These effects, according to Breggin (see, www.breggin.com/Ritalinprnews.html 2000) include the child becoming 'zombie like', withdrawn and depressed. He adds that they can also produce drug-induced behavioural disorders such as psychosis, mania, drug abuse and addiction.

A small number of neuroimaging studies (e.g. using electroencephalography) have found a relationship between abnormalities in the striatal regions of the brain and some individuals with ADHD (Cooper and Bilton 1999). However, Barkley (1997) suggests that neuroimaging research has failed to establish evidence of brain damage as a cause of ADHD. He argues that where brain abnormalities have been found to correlate with ADHD they result from abnormal neurological development.

Barkley (1997) offers a cognitive model to explain ADHD that emphasises a lack of impulse control, and problems with self-regulation. Put simply an individual with ADHD lacks the ability to maintain focus on longer-term goals because immediate goals overpower them. This is not to suggest that such individuals are not consciously aware of the value of longer-term goals. For example, a child may well recognise the advantages of sharing and taking turns in order to be socially accepted within a group, but this goal may be overtaken by a desire to dominate a particular activity, even if such behaviour results in the group rejecting him or her in the future. For Barkley, this lack of impulse control results, in part, from a lack of development in the brain's executive systems or those processes which enable an individual to self-regulate and form goals. Barkley identifies four main components to these systems – working memory, internalised speech, motivation/emotional appraisal, and behaviour synthesis. As we develop, our experiences add to: our memory, which we may subsequently call upon as reference for our future responses; our experience of language and the nature of internalised meanings and images which should become more diverse and informed over time; our ability to separate emotions from cognition and to put them into perspective; and our ability to engage in a review of our previous behavioural responses and their effectiveness. The key to engaging these functions effectively is the ability to wait sufficiently long enough for them to come into play. Barkley argues that in children with ADHD, the ability to wait is medically impaired and, as a consequence, these executive functions are not activated or are activated too late. As a result there is less opportunity for such children to refine them which makes social encounters problematic. The use of medication allows sufficient time for executive functioning to come into play. Different cognitive explanations of ADHD have been offered by other psychologists including, 'delay aversion' (Sonuga-Barke *et al.* 1992) and the 'cognitive-energetic model' of ADHD (Sergeant 1995).

Other researchers have looked at differences in the attributional style of children with ADHD compared with children who do not. Research carried out by Chaney and Bugental (1982) demonstrated that the attributions of hyperactive children were different from other children. Hyperactive children were less likely to see the value of effort in their explanations of why particular outcomes had occurred, suggesting that they perceived themselves as having less control over such outcomes. Attribution theory is concerned with the explanations we have about the *perceived* (as opposed to real) causes of our own and other people's behaviour. For example, if a child is offensive to a teacher in a classroom then that teacher might conclude the child is behaving that way because he or she does not respect others, or perhaps is just being 'nasty'. Which explanation is selected depends on a combination of previous experiences with this pupil (and other pupils), along with what was happening at the time and how the teacher was feeling. Different explanations result in different responses from the teacher. Pupils also engage in this process making attributions about their own behaviours and those of their teachers. Subsequent responses from both parties, based on these perceptions, may create an ongoing negative cycle exacerbating the negative behaviours and reinforcing initial perceptions.

What becomes evident from examining research into ADHD is a tendency by many contributors to focus on single factor explanations, many of which are located within the child. This emphasis persists despite many of the same researchers simultaneously espousing the biopsychosocial nature of ADHD. The narrow focusing of some research activity arises in part because of the difficulties in trying to incorporate all possible variables into a research design and also because of the traditional emphases of different professional groups.

Research issue 1.1 Understanding theoretical perspectives

Detailed examination of professional perspectives and explanations for a specific SEN can be useful, not just as part of a literature review but also as a means of engaging with the operational definition for your own study and providing a basis for comparing your own findings with those of others.

Barriers to professional cooperation

In searching to unravel the often contradictory nature of explanations from different professional groups, we turn our attention to their structure, control and operation. Two fundamental areas where differences appear most evident are, firstly, philosophical differences which include ethical codes, training and working practices and secondly, differences in power and status which influence access to and control of information.

Philosophical differences

As many reports into children who are 'looked after' have revealed (DOH 1991) a significant number of professionals charged with the education and development of young people have a poor record when it comes to providing a coordinated response to the needs of their charges. This has resulted in the uneconomic use of resources and in some cases the abuse of young people.

Difficulties can also occur because of conflicting perspectives on child development, including the nature of intelligence and the level of decision-making permitted to children. In order to understand why those charged with providing for the needs of a common 'client' have such difficulty coordinating their interventions we need to examine their basic philosophy and, in turn, their training. Teachers, social workers, doctors and psychologists for instance, undergo very different training, operate under different codes of practice and they use very different language to explain similar things. 'Professional' language (jargon) used to describe specific concepts and constructs is agreed within one discipline. However, it may mystify not only parents and children but also other professionals outside that discipline who define similar concepts in different ways. Indeed the way in which different professionals refer to those they 'serve' adds to the confusion. Doctors have 'patients', teachers have 'pupils' and social workers have 'clients'. These very different descriptors often describe the same individual but carry with them differing implications, expectations and approaches. Similarly, 'treatment', 'care', 'educating' and 'empowerment' mean different things to different professional groups. Teachers, unlike social workers and doctors, are required to work with both groups of pupils and individuals and be both *an authority* and *in authority*, making very different demands on them.

Power and status

Professionals are often perceived to be ordered hierarchically – a hierarchy which relates directly to power, accountability and access. Those of you who have attended a court will no doubt be aware of the power and status differences among those present and how in many instances decision-making power is usually inversely proportional to involvement with the client – contrast a high court judge with a residential key worker! In the field of SEN such differences are perhaps most obvious at case conferences or reviews where a number of professionals often attend. This can represent an interesting group dynamic as different individuals put forward explanations and recommendations, which reflect a very different understanding of the learning or behavioural difficulty under scrutiny. These differences are also evident in decision making about who and what might be researched and by whom. Different ethical codes and levels of training may empower or marginalise certain professional groups. Some measures are only available for use by a particular profession (e.g. psychologists and certain intelligence tests) which then excludes other groups (e.g. teachers) from pursuing particular research methods.

Research issue 1.2 Professional status and supporting pupils' needs
Given the very different status of those involved, how can we be sure that pupils' needs are best served? Is it reasonable to assume that the 'senior' professional or most qualified group knows what a particular child 'needs' better than someone working at the 'chalk face' or a parent?

Contemporary issues in education theory and practice – the bigger picture

In recent years we have witnessed a growing interest in raising the 'quality' of schooling through the use of performance indicators. Research in this field has taken two main directions. One of these approaches is concerned with school effectiveness research which claims to measure the performance of pupils and schools in terms of progress through the key stages. The second is concerned with school improvement, that is making changes within schools to make them more 'effective'. A third area which has received attention reflects changes outside schooling and is concerned ostensibly with recognising and valuing the contribution of consumers (in this case pupils and their parents) to the quality of schooling. This area reflects a growing trend in society at large for service providers to be accountable for their actions.

Measuring performance – School Effectiveness Research

The most common approach to this type of research is *quantitative* (see Chapter 4 for more details) which usually involves making comparative measures of academic performance between individuals, groups and institutions (Reynolds *et al.* 1994). However, these comparative measures often seem unhelpful and difficult to apply to schools where there are large proportions of pupils with special educational needs, since the rate of progress for some groups is significantly slower than their peers – a factor which can result in lower performance marker levels for the school as a whole. This method of measuring school and student performance has therefore raised objections from those schools with high levels of pupils with special educational needs who argued that the *relative* gain across a range of characteristics, including social as well as academic development, is a fairer way of evaluating the value added to a young person's education. Consider for instance, pupils with behavioural difficulties, where the concern is for their academic advancement at the same time as improving their social behaviour: which of the two should be measured first and how is the improvement in social behaviour analysed alongside academic performance markers? This situation is further exacerbated in many special schools and units, where exam performance is usually significantly lower than in mainstream schools, and where academic input has to be balanced with a range of therapeutic and medical interventions.

In order to try and integrate these multiple and diverse factors sophisticated statistical techniques have been developed such as *multilevel modelling* (see Kreft and de Leeuw 1998). These techniques have made the measurement of 'value added' potentially fairer since they can incorporate different types of variables at different hierarchical levels. Thus measurement takes place at the individual, group and institutional level, while controlling for various effects such as socio-economic status. Differences in relative performance are often demonstrated diagrammatically by plotting scores from different schools and measuring differences in gradient of the line between them – as opposed to merely looking at final overall performance in, say, GCSE examinations.

Raising standards – School Improvement Research

In contrast to the school effectiveness research, school improvement research has focused on qualitative methods (see Chapter 4 for more details) – usually in the form of *case studies*. If a school is identified as having difficulties in a particular area, researchers try to identify what is the cause. Some approaches look at management structures within the school or the organisational climate (school ethos). Others have examined the relationship between (or dynamics of) *input* to the school (staff characteristics, pupil characteristics and/or physical structures), *processes* (teaching and learning, pastoral activity) and *outcomes* (academic performance, social behaviour, disaffection). See Gray *et al.* (1999) for examples of school improvement studies.

Recognising the views of the consumer – Pupil Voice Research

Although previously receiving only limited attention, the pupil voice movement is concerned with incorporating the views of young people into the organisation, structure and decision-making activities of schools. Researchers in this field have used a variety of measures including quantitative – usually in the form of attitude and perception scales (e.g. Chaplain 2000c) – and qualitative measures such as interviews individually or in groups. Findings are often more familiar than novel (Barber 1994; Blatchford 1996). Notable consistencies are the lack of respect pupils feel they receive from teachers (often as opposed to adults in general, since many young people are used to working with adults outside of schools who treat them differently); questioning the lack of instrumentality in schools (i.e., the non-relevance to their futures, of much of what they are required to learn); lack of autonomy and decision making powers, and lack of appropriate support (Chaplain 2000c). Despite claims to the contrary, being asked their opinion is often a novel event for pupils since schools are historically not places where all pupils are encouraged to express their opinion. Freeman (1988) argued that the reason for this is that we perceive pupils as incompetent and thus their opinion is of little value. This situation is further exacerbated in the case of pupils who have special educational needs since they are perceived as even less competent and, as such, less likely to have a worthwhile contribution to make.

What is largely missing from the research literature is the voice of disabled people – there are relatively few disabled people in academic positions, for example. Some debates have focused on 'voice' (Clough and Barton 1995a) and the ways in which disabled people's views may be fully represented. Questions have also been raised regarding the reliability of offering individual accounts as being representative of a 'group', as Dyson (1998) points out:

. . . grounding the truth claim of a piece of research on the notion of 'voice' involves making decisions about what constitutes 'voice' of an individual, or which voice within a group is representative of that group. (p. 9)

Dyson goes on to remind us that for 'every voice heard, another is silenced' and that for every oppressed group that is brought to the foreground for attention, 'another's oppression is denied or ignored' (p. 10). Thus, it is important to be aware of the unintended consequences of a particular course of action as well as those which are intended.

Children's rights and professional responsibility

While schools continue to manage pupils' social behaviour alongside empowering their transition to independence there has been considerable change in the legal status of young people and indeed changes to their rights. A central principle of the Children Act (1989) was paramountcy of the child, whereby the best interests of the child was to be the starting point in any decision making on their behalf by professionals (e.g. teachers and social workers) responsible for their development and care.

Extending issues from this debate are considerations such as who should authorise the involvement of young people in research. Ethically speaking, the young person should have the right to say *no* to any investigation of them or their circumstances. However, it is often still more common to ask parents or teachers *in loco parentis* for this permission. While this may seem acceptable, there still remains the issue of consent and ownership of data over time. An adolescent may agree (along with her parents) to the filming of her behaviour when she is 13, but what if at the age of 18 she questions the activity; arguing that she was 'pressured' into becoming involved or that her best interests were not served or that she was experiencing considerable stress at the time and that involvement with the research project made matters worse? The central issue here is, who owns the data – the pupil(s), their parents or the researcher – and for how long? In the context of ever-expanding litigation one needs to be aware as a researcher of some of the potential difficulties, especially when working with vulnerable client groups.

Teachers as researchers

The changing face of the research community – a new orthodoxy?

Educational research was the target of much criticism during the 1990s. Reports appeared attacking academic researchers for the use of impenetrable jargon and the lack of relevance to current educational policies and initiatives (see for instance, Hargreaves 1996). At the same time, researchers in universities were being examined and classified by a new mechanism known as the Research Assessment Exercise (RAE) – the quantity and 'quality' of research produced over a four year period was linked to the level of funding given to the institution for further research. Higher status research, i.e. that which received most credit from the RAE was that published in refereed academic journals, as opposed to producing materials of direct practical value to schools.

Alongside these developments was the expansion of funding for school-based researchers such as the DfEE's Best Practice Research programmes, set up in 2000 to enable teachers to undertake small scale studies in priority areas in order to spread best practice and improve teaching and learning in classrooms (www.dfee.gov.uk/bprs). This development, together with the RAE, was instrumental in controlling the shape and direction of research as well as how it should be carried out and by whom. The degree to which such division of effort is an effective way of advancing knowledge and practice is questionable.

To what extent this 'change of emphasis' was novel or represented an attack on the established orthodoxy is not clear. Educational research had already been moving in the direction of incorporating school-based research by teachers as a direct means of solving problems and improving teaching and learning in school for some time, in particular through action research (Stenhouse 1983).

Research issue 1.3 The organisation and control of research
How should the balance between academic researchers and teacher researchers be addressed and where should overall control lie? How do we address the issues of knowledge, insight and skills? Is it always most effective to have those most directly involved with a problem identifying and/or researching it? How might we generate time within teachers' timetables to allow the pursuit of research and how much time should be dedicated to research?

Approaches to educational research – the need to be 'useful'

Cohen and Manion (2000, p. 3) point out that 'education, educational research, politics and decision-making are inextricably intertwined'. Educational research is commonly perceived to have the purpose of necessarily improving education. The Teacher Training Agency statement on research (TTA 1998) outlines a 12-point strategy for using research to inform and improve professional practice, including the criterion of 'usefulness' to head teachers, teachers and policy makers as part of any assessment of quality.

A central issue in the debate regarding the 'usefulness' of educational research relates to methodology. One important contrast is between 'positivist' (or 'normative') approaches, which attempt to discover general laws governing aspects of human thinking and behaviour, and 'interpretive' (or 'idiographic') approaches which attempt to understand the relationship between people's idiosyncratic experiences, beliefs, feelings and actions in everyday social situations. The positivist approach, whose origins lie in the natural sciences, considers social reality as ultimately knowable, observable, predictable and in many respects measurable. The interpretive approach sees human behaviour as only understandable through investigation of the meaning and purposes people give to their actions in particular circumstances.

The differences between these two approaches have been carefully and critically discussed elsewhere. (see, for example, Cohen and Manion 2000; Hitchcock and Hughes 1995). Briefly, the fundamental distinction ties in the theoretical aim. A positivist or normative approach in educational research aims to extend theoretical knowledge by formulating hypotheses about behaviour and then testing the reliability of these hypotheses using evidence about relationships between variables in the teaching and learning process – where possible controlling all but those variables being measured. In contrast, an interpretive approach aims to build theories about behaviour grounded in the perspectives of the people involved, using evidence about people's understandings and motives in different circumstances. So a positivist approach to understanding 'dyslexia' might involve measuring the educational attainments and classroom behaviour of groups of pupils placed in different classes using different approaches to teaching reading – testing the hypotheses for example, that pupils identified as dyslexic concentrate and learn more effectively with a 'phonics' approach. In contrast, an interpretive approach to the same topic might involve the teacher and pupils in observations, discussions and interviews about the day-to-day classroom experiences of assessment, teaching and learning to read, gathering evidence over time about the apparent connections between different aspects of the processes of classroom learning and pupils' reading progress.

Some research methods tend to be associated with one approach or the other. For example, experiments and large-scale surveys on their own will tend to be used in positivist research, while participant observation, discussion and the combination of such methods will tend to be used in interpretive research (see Chapters 3 and 4 for more detailed discussion of specific research methods). However, no method is exclusive to one approach. For example, interviewing may be used in either positivist or interpretive research – it depends on how the questions are planned and how the answers are analysed.

One of the main points relevant to research by teachers relates to the perceived role of the researcher and the people 'being researched': positivist researchers are seen as standing apart from the situation and view the people involved as observable 'subjects' of study, while interpretive researchers are usually inextricably involved in the situation along with all the other 'participants'. There are clearly advantages and disadvantages in both stances. A positivist approach will tend to involve large samples of people identified by their representative characteristics (e.g. gender, age, attainment level, type of school placement, etc.) while interpretive approaches, given the required level of involvement, tend to be smaller-scale studies of known individuals and groups of people in particular situations – although small studies *can* be positivist and large studies *can* be interpretive.

We might argue that *both* research approaches have a place in educational research today and that neither is sufficient for understanding and improving education. Indeed much research incorporates more than one method (triangulation). However we have to recognise the underlying contradictions between the two approaches in the view of human understanding and behaviour.

A third approach, and one which is of particular relevance to the empowerment of pupils with SEN, was the development of 'emancipatory' research which questioned the usefulness and effectiveness of both positivist and interpretive approaches when researching oppressed groups such as the disabled. Emancipatory research is concerned with empowering oppressed groups by changing the balance of the relationship between researchers and researched. According to Oliver (1992):

> The issue then for the emancipatory research paradigm is not how to empower people but, once people have decided to empower themselves, precisely what research can then do to facilitate this process. This does then mean that the social relations of research production do have to be fundamentally changed; researchers have to learn how to put their knowledge and skills at the disposal of their research subjects, for them to use in whatever ways they choose. (p. 111)

In this paradigm, control of the research is in the hands of those being researched, as opposed to the researcher. Furthermore, this change in control is based on three fundamentals – reciprocity, gain and empowerment (Oliver 1997). While other approaches, such as action research, have resulted in participants (e.g. teachers) joining the research community and contributing directly to research knowledge, emancipatory research argues that no one should be overlooked in the first place. Oliver goes on to further distinguish the fundamental difference between participatory and emancipatory research as:

> Participatory and action research is about improving the existing social and material relations of research production; not challenging and ultimately eradicating them. (p. 26)

Emancipatory research therefore, represents a radical departure from the more established positivist and interpretive approaches.

Research issue 1.4 Selecting an appropriate methodology

The arguments surrounding which methodology best represents the 'reality' of a situation has been commonplace among the research community for many years and looks set to continue waxing and waning between the two basic approaches. Often a particular paradigm takes centre stage for a while only to then be criticised by proponents of the second approach who in turn come under scrutiny of the first and so on. However, the central issue should always be – what is it we wish to find out? And, what methodology would best facilitate this?

Bias in the research process: faulty thinking or normal behaviour?

One common bias in the western world is to over-emphasise personal disposition rather than social context when looking to explain why others behave the way they do. In other words if someone is not behaving the way we believe they should we are more likely to blame them for their actions as opposed to blaming the situation (e.g. the quality of teaching or classroom organisation). One reason for this is, that if we blame the situation then we blame ourselves, since we are part of that situation. In a classroom this is exacerbated since teachers are expected to be in control of such factors. This process applies at both the individual and social level. For example, Mugny and Carugati's (1989) research on social representations of intelligence, suggests groups of experienced teachers may come to agree about 'within-child' causes of learning difficulties because doing so enables the establishment and protection of professional identity (see also Croll and Moses 2000).

Research issue 1.5 Bias in approaching research projects

It is important to be aware of the 'natural' and learned biases in our thinking when preparing for and engaging in a research project. What we select to research is likely to be influenced by our existing beliefs, as is our choice of methodology and method. Someone who finds maths easy is perhaps more likely (though not necessarily) to find themselves drawn into using quantitative techniques.

Involving teachers in educational research

There is a growing belief that teachers' professional knowledge has a place in the development of a good education system. As the most recent version of the National Curriculum (QCA 1999) states:

> Teachers individually and collectively, have to reappraise their teaching in response to the changing needs of economic, social and cultural change. Education only flourishes if it successfully adapts to the demands of the time. (p. 13)

The implication is, that knowledge about the 'demands and needs of the time' – relating both to pupils' needs and to wider social and economic factors – has to be a factor in teachers' decision making.

The involvement of teachers in this process is now expected to begin during initial training as part of the process often seen as one aspect of becoming a 'reflective teacher'. The current guidelines in England and Wales (DfEE 1998c) require newly qualified teachers to 'engage with research findings relating to children's development, teaching and learning' (pp. 9,10,16). The emphasis appears to be on understanding other people's research findings, however there is an established strong case for qualified teachers to research for themselves topics and issues relevant to their everyday work. Arguments in support of teacher/researchers include: individual professional development (Stenhouse 1983); institutional development (Halsall 1998); extending and improving educational research (Hargreaves 1996); and improved understanding of, in particular, special educational needs (Ainscow 1998).

Research issue 1.6 Motives for engaging in research
We might make a distinction between professional reasons for teachers to engage in research as above, and personal motives, which may range from career development to the improvement of teaching and learning; increasing personal/professional knowledge; empowerment in school; evaluation; interest/enjoyment; participation with colleagues; etc. – and any combination of these. The interplay between these different interests can lead to tensions between staff.

There is empirical support for the positive outcomes of teacher research. For example, Vulliamy and Webb (1992) found from their questionnaires and interviews with seven cohorts of teacher researchers on masters degree courses that there were important contributions to personal and professional development, changing classroom practice and influencing school policy. However, there are also problems – particularly with the use of time, confidence, skill and organisation attitudes of senior management, upheavals, use and generalisability of findings evaluation and dissemination of findings etc. (p. 16).

Further, Robson (1993) points out that when practitioners are engaged in research, they no longer tend to devise their own projects primarily out of individual interest.

> The move is towards study relevant to the professional setting, in part at least determined by the agenda and concerns of that setting. Reduction in individual freedom is balanced by an increasing likelihood of implementation, and of additional resources and time for the practitioner-researcher. (p. 446)

In spite of such problems there is general agreement that teachers need to keep abreast of new developments in education, including findings from educational and allied human service research. Active engagement in school-based research offers teachers a means of obtaining a deeper understanding of teaching and learning in the context of the constant changes to policy and practice and social structures. Moreover the dissemination of teachers' research findings at a local or national level complements published findings from studies carried out by academic researchers and other professional colleagues. In total, we would argue that this diverse body of educational research provides a growing knowledge base for making educational decisions which have a real influence on teaching and learning.

CHAPTER 2

Key research issues in SEN

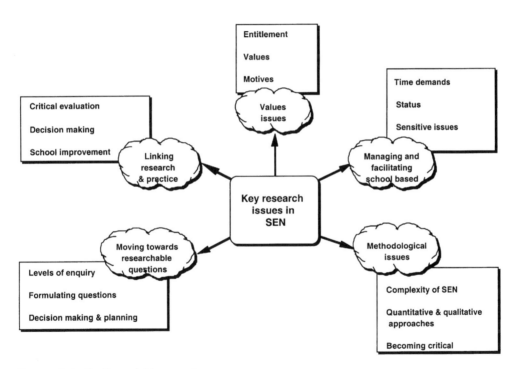

Figure 2.1 Outline of Chapter 2

In Chapter 1 we raised a number of issues which appear regularly as points of debate for educational research, and which have particular implications for school-based research in the areas of SEN and inclusion. We now consider these issues under five broad headings (Figure 2.1):

- linking research and practice;

- values issues;
- managing and facilitating school-based research;
- methodological issues;
- moving towards researchable questions.

Certain questions arise throughout the chapter: What is actually relevant and 'researchable' by teachers, given the activities, changes and interactions occurring at different levels of the educational system? How can school-based research be inclusive and meaningful for all concerned, given the power and status differentials and the alternative perspectives influencing the identification and provision for children with SEN? How can teachers' research best contribute to knowledge, understanding and effective problem-solving, given the different paradigms of educational research and the debates about the links between educational theory and practice?

Any school-based investigation will involve making some difficult decisions about research strategies and methodology. Yet this does not make research impossible. There is a need to make similarly difficult decisions in responding to the intrinsic dilemmas of teaching from day-to-day. In the end, the professional skills and judgements used in teaching pupils with SEN and considering inclusion will also underpin the decision-making involved in school-based research.

Linking research and practice

Many problems and dilemmas for both teaching and research arise because teachers are pulled in different directions. Teachers need to respond quickly to the pupils who are in immediate danger of losing out in their learning, but this aspect of teaching takes place alongside longer-term developments in education and society, aimed at improving education for *all* pupils. If the broad aims of educational research are both to respond to teachers' needs and to build a body of knowledge about educational processes, then we need to ask how needs and problems are defined, how knowledge accumulates and how the body of knowledge can be accepted as 'useful'. Such questions are familiar to anyone working in the field of SEN and inclusion, where professionals, parents and pupils have to find a way of communicating and, as discussed in Chapter 1, where people's expectations, rights and responsibilities have to be examined critically.

One of the strongest arguments for school-based research is that teachers' knowledge and understanding about education develops through activity and discussion in the contexts where teaching and learning are taking place – i.e. as members of a 'community of practice' (Lave and Wenger 1991). So questions about how research can be useful to teachers may be better expressed in terms of how useful knowledge and understanding can be accumulated *without* school-based research by teachers. Teacher research would appear to be a very good way to integrate educational research and professional practice, especially when the topic of study emerges from current concerns or issues which have to be dealt with in school (e.g. how to allocate resources to most effect, or how to improve pupils' maths attainment in Year 3). Yet the school-based investigation of such topics is rarely straightforward. It is difficult even with 'local knowledge' to take account of the many interacting factors involved. Furthermore, it has been recognised that there is rarely a direct linear relationship between research findings and the implications for professional practice, given the frequent need to reconcile different political views and values – often through a process of bargaining rather than logic (Tizard 1991).

Decision-making, evidence-based practice and critical evaluation

One of the themes emerging in recent writing about SEN, is that teachers inevitably make decisions in a state of uncertainty about the outcome. There is little possibility of reliable, recipe-like matching of an intervention to a 'type' of SEN, even though there has been much theoretical and practical effort in this direction. Consequently, many researchers are interested in the means by which good teaching decisions are made by all involved, as well as the apparent effectiveness of the available teaching options. In their discussion of 'decision making in uncertainty', Pijl and van den Bos (1998, p. 114) comment on the problems arising from the relative failure to find robust theoretical models to apply to learning problems. As an alternative to the potentially misleading effects of using only personal experience and intuition as a basis for making teaching decisions, they propose that decision-making should be seen as a regulatory cycle, with phases and rules, in which the goal is action rather than prediction. The evaluation of action is used to adjust or regulate the process in relation to the original goals and intentions. This is a fundamental professional skill (or art) rather than a simple, mechanical process. As Bayliss (1998) comments, practitioners do not see the working world as a place where 'simple problems have simple solutions':

> If we are dealing with complexity, we (as practitioners and researchers) must accept that change, mutability and non-predictability are natural parts of dynamic systems and that 'certainty' is only provided by an artificial view of the world. A theory of special education must provide practitioners with the confidence to accept that uncertainty. (p. 78)

This decision-making cycle mirrors the concept of 'evidence-based practice' – a notion which has been central to government thinking in recent years, with the now familiar references to school performance data, target setting and evaluation. The government's guidance on target setting for pupils with SEN (DfEE 1998d, p. 6) refers to the 'School Improvement Cycle', which involves the following procedure for making links between data about pupil achievement and day-to-day teaching and learning:

1. How well are we doing?
2. How do we compare with similar schools?
3. What more should we aim to achieve this year?
4. What must we do to make it happen?
5. Taking action and reviewing progress.

This type of evidence about progress towards pre-set targets, together with the official attention to disseminating and building on research findings about 'best practice' (DfEE 1998a) has found its place in current thinking about SEN and inclusion. Yet there are some problems in seeing this as 'evidence-based practice' in the way that might apply in other areas such as medicine, for the following reasons: first, educational targets which are limited to the observable and measurable aspects of children's behaviour and learning cut out large chunks of valuable educational experience, knowledge and understanding; and second, 'best practice' in education often has a strong contextual dimension, in that it is largely identified in specific settings. This sense of real-life context provides an authenticity and a richness of meaning and detail, but the generalisation to other contexts and cultures can only be approached through cumulative professional discourse (Bassey, 1999). Problems of definition also appear when gathering evidence at national and international level. For instance, in his discussion of evidence-based practice, Evans (2000, p. 69) notes the difficulties of comparing international research on SEN and inclusion owing to the 'substantial differences between countries in the way special needs issues are conceptualised and discussed'.

Values issues

Part of the problem in linking research with practice concerns the values embedded in the definitions and discussions of SEN and inclusion. The 'valuing' aspect of evaluation is sometimes ignored in the drive to gather evidence about whether aims and targets have been met. Yet the field of SEN and inclusion is permeated by values which inevitably inform evaluations of current practice and new initiatives. The National Curriculum (NC) for England and Wales (QCA 1999) states that there is a broad consensus on the 'enduring' values which underpin the school curriculum and the work of schools:

These include valuing ourselves, our families and other relationships, the wider groups to which we belong, the diversity in our society and the environment in which we live'. (p. 10)

These values are said to be 'so fundamental that they may appear unexceptional' (p. 147), although it is also recognised that:

> Their demanding nature is demonstrated both by our collective failure consistently to live up to them, and the moral challenge which acting on them in practice entails. (p. 147)

We might, of course, question the degree to which such values and purposes *are* explicitly shared within society, but, in any case, the values as given above deserve attention alongside the stated purposes of the NC (p. 12–13):

- to establish an entitlement;
- to establish standards;
- to promote continuity and coherence;
- to promote public understanding.

There are tensions here between, say, establishing a curriculum entitlement for all pupils, and establishing a set of standards and measurable targets for school performance and certain individual pupils: if the targets are too narrowly based on basic skills, then pupils whose strengths lie elsewhere may be devalued and excluded; if pupils' diverse strengths are recognised and cultivated then basic school targets may not be achieved.

In his discussion of inclusion, Norwich (2000, p. 17–8) argues that:

> . . . because we do not have simple and single ideas and values about educational excellence . . . we cannot avoid complex ideas about inclusion and effectiveness. This arises in part from contradictions or dilemmas about educational values themselves and in part from limitations of our current capabilities to resolve problems in education and the wider society. We have multiple values in education which cannot be assumed to be mutually compatible in full.

These intrinsic dilemmas about values and purposes can quickly surface in investigating SEN and inclusion in school, although Armstrong *et al.* (1998, p. 32) suggest that:

> . . . much of the research in special education . . . is loosely and perhaps misleadingly centred upon unexplicated and unproblematised humanitarian values such as 'care', 'equal opportunities', 'access', 'school improvement'.

Some researchers make values explicit, especially when taking a critical or emancipatory stance (e.g. in aiming to challenge social inequality). Clough and Barton (1995b, p. 5) argue that exposing the assumptions and values of the researcher will:

. . . enhance the claim of the work to make morally and politically important statements. This includes the extent to which the participants found the experience of the research process to be challenging and enabling.

Not all researchers would place themselves in the emancipatory paradigm, but all research and evaluation projects will gain from taking some steps in this direction by exploring the values underpinning the choice of research topic and methodology, the decision-making procedures and the criteria which are used to judge progress and success (see Research tip 2.1 and Chapter 4).

Research tip 2.1 Exploring values
Exploring values in research on SEN and inclusion can be a research topic in its own right, but it is also intrinsic to any school-based research project. One way to include an exploration of values, while planning and carrying out research in school, is to make explicit connections to the values expressed in policy documents produced in school, including the public statements of aims in the prospectus. To what extent are the espoused values commonly shared by staff and pupils? How are they represented in practice? How do they inform the questions, methods and interpretations in the research project?

Alternatively, in exploring values it might be appropriate to introduce a framework for discussion which links to the school development plan. For example, the Index for Inclusion (CSIE 2000), sent to schools by the DfEE, includes a set of materials which focus on building inclusive school cultures, policies and practices. It provides some indicators of what might be seen as 'inclusive values' (p. 46) and related questions which could be addressed in school (p. 58). These are inevitably thought-provoking for school staff teams, given the genuine dilemmas and differences of opinion about the aims and possibilities of inclusion in the current educational system.

Managing and facilitating school-based research

In practical terms, embedded values can become very clear in the ways that research is planned and carried out in school. Values can be evident in the status research is given, the ways in which it is supported, the topics of investigation and the involvement of colleagues, children and parents. Teachers' personal and professional motives for carrying out school-based research on SEN may be strongly influenced by the perceived status of the research topic – both in school and beyond. Within school, this reflects the importance given to SEN and inclusion in terms of the relative emphasis on helping individuals and groups of pupils as part of whole-school development. If teaching pupils with SEN is generally marginalised in school then school-based research in this area is likely to be seen as peripheral to the main business of teaching. However, the perceived 'usefulness' of a research project can influence the personal feelings of teacher colleagues and the school's policies and practice. Research which helps to solve obvious and immediate problems in school will gain in status, whatever the underlying views about SEN and inclusion – although its effects may be limited.

The status of SEN as a research topic is also affected by factors beyond individual schools. Teacher research networks or teachers' involvement with externally funded research projects can invest a project with credibility and value, often via the concrete impact of additional funding coming into school. School-based research linked to a diploma or higher degree may similarly add status, but this can depend on the perceptions of an individual teacher's motivations for further study. Colleagues' reactions may range from enthusiastic support to tolerance to active rejection, depending on the staff relationships already in existence and the degree to which the teacher's motives are seen to reflect altruism, personal interest or naked ambition. This can be further complicated by inter-professional misunderstandings and rivalries and by differences of opinion about the rights of involvement for those directly involved in SEN decision-making – including pupils and parents.

In discussing the status of school-based research by teachers we are also raising questions about the *control* of research and knowledge in professional practice. Part of the problem here lies in the combination of different issues arising in teaching and research on SEN and inclusion. Dyson (1998, p. 11) contends that 'the powerful disability movement in the UK and beyond' has been 'bundled' in education with other issues about low attainment and disaffection. As a result general concerns about responding to pupils' individual differences may come into conflict with concerns about the specific needs of certain groups of pupils, and the associated inequalities in provision. There is therefore the possibility of disputes and bias *within* the arena of SEN, and we need to question the degree to which teaching and research both reflect and influence different positions and interests. We might, for instance compare the extensive research efforts and resources directed towards dyslexia/ADHD with those addressing moderate learning difficulties and low attainment. It is possible to prevent serious conflicts between school colleagues through sharing ideas, discussing intentions and reporting findings to everyone involved, and by collaborating where possible (see Research tips 2.2 – 2.5, below). However, we would not want to underplay the potential problems in giving attention to certain topics and investigations when school-based research itself is still largely seen as a personal choice rather than a professional expectation for teachers.

> **Research tip 2.2 The responsibility to disseminate research findings**
> Stenhouse (1983) defined research as 'systematic investigation made public'. Some problems with the status of school-based research can arise because it is not clear who the research is for and what is going to be gained. Ideally, the early plans for a research project will include the intentions for the dissemination and publication of findings. This can be a good way to prevent misconceptions and gain encouragement and support from colleagues, children and parents.
>
> Beyond school, the publication and dissemination of the findings of school-based research will extend the awareness and status of individual school-based projects, and this can also lead to valuable information exchange, collaborations and larger projects. However the routes for publishing teachers' school-based research findings are not clearly signposted. We return to this in Chapter 5 with some ideas and

Some of the practical problems for teachers in carrying out school-based research and implementing changes in response, were acknowledged in Chapter 1. Problems commonly arise in terms of time management, pressure from other national and local initiatives, attitudes of senior management (especially the head teacher), general school ethos, and the degree to which the research is private or shared with other staff (compared to teaching in general) (Vulliamy and Webb 1992, p. 17–8). It has to be recognised that for most teachers, at the time of writing, research is something additional to their normal work, so school-based research can be difficult without formal acknowledgement and encouragement from senior management, together with practical support (see Research tip 2.3).

> **Research tip 2.3 Valuing and facilitating teacher research in school**
> The concrete demonstration of support from senior management is central to carrying a school-based project through to completion. This might include the provision of non-contact time, appropriate technology for data collection and analysis, and administrative facilities. Conversely, a research project carried out by a member of the senior management team will need to be examined for its practical implications for more junior teaching staff, particularly if they are asked to gather data in their own lessons (e.g. observations, questionnaires, discussions, etc.).
>
> Additional support required for data gathering and analysis may be provided through training and consultation with more experienced colleagues in school, in the LEA or higher education.
>
> One of the most successful ways of managing school-based research is to make it a whole-school priority and ensure that all teachers are involved. For example, in the Effective Learning Project (a teacher research network, Flutter *et al.* 1998), one primary head teacher took each class in turn so that every teacher could be involved in interviewing pupils – rather than limiting the project to certain teachers and classes.

Further professional issues arise when a school-based research project tackles 'difficult' issues (see Research tip 2.4). There are few 'easy' issues in the field of SEN and inclusion, but there are undoubtedly some particularly sensitive and problematic topics in certain settings. Consider, for example, the implications of focusing research on one pupil, a group of pupils, a whole class, or the whole school. If the focus is on certain pupils or groups, then how and why are they selected? If the focus is on the whole school (e.g. to investigate 'inclusion'), then how can such a complex organisation be studied in a way that is valid and acceptable to staff and pupils? The specific topic of research can also be problematic. For instance, researching access for pupils with physical disabilities may (but not always) be less controversial than investigations of emotional and behavioural difficulties, bullying or racism.

Research tip 2.4 Tackling difficult issues in school-based research

Research questions may tactfully by-pass a known problem (e.g. the teaching capabilities of oneself or other members of staff) or they may tackle them head-on, depending on the quality of staff relationships and the level of school development. A useful rule of thumb is that school-based research should not involve anything that would compromise professional judgement – especially regarding the teacher's responsibility to the pupils. However, it is hard to separate the decision to engage in research from an interest in carrying out an investigation that is genuinely open-minded, honest and truthful (even while asking 'whose truth?').

One response to such dilemmas is to see school-based research as developmental or modular. It can be legitimate and effective to begin with a small, focused study, and then to present the findings to colleagues or an external 'critical friend' before going further. This acts both as a check on one's own interpretations and as a means to involve other staff in a meaningful way. In this way difficult issues can be tackled through research in a way that is both methodologically valid and professionally appropriate. In Chapter 4 we suggest some ways of carrying out research in stages.

Difficult issues can be highlighted when school-based research involves colleagues in some way. As discussed in Chapter 1, there can be significant tensions between professionals, with problems generated by the different perspectives on pupils' behaviour and learning. In talking about SEN and inclusion, people may even be using a different language which requires translation. So 'useful' research has to be approached in way that takes account of the language of SEN and the relevance of people's perceptions and attitudes. Pragmatically, there is a need to examine the language of SEN in order to facilitate communication and collaboration between pupils, parents, teachers, other professionals, researchers and others involved. This includes the dissemination and use of research findings.

There are further questions about 'expertise' in assessment and intervention, which may influence both teachers' confidence in setting up a school-based research project and their colleagues' perceptions of this enterprise (see Research tip 2.5). A research project cannot be allowed to compromise other aspects of the professional relationships which allow teaching to take place. The ideal outcome would be for it to enrich professional teamwork, possibly in unexpected ways.

Research tip 2. 5 Involving colleagues

Given the nature of SEN and inclusion, it is hard to avoid involving colleagues in the research and it can be very helpful to do so. It is important to clarify the nature of colleagues' involvement in the project, especially whether they are collaborators, participants or users. This may involve:

- an initial negotiation which takes account of how colleagues want to be involved;
- finding out whether they are already involved in a similar project, or have been in the past;
- discussing and agreeing arrangements for reporting and dissemination of findings.

Finally, and summing up a lot of what has gone before, ethical considerations are central to school-based research. This involves not only considering how to gain the informed consent and participation of pupils, parents and other adults for one's own project, but also understanding the views of the people who are more often the researched than the researchers (Kitchin 2000). There is a need to take care about the use of language throughout the project. As discussed in Chapter 1, there are sensitive personal and political issues about the use of terms to describe people and schools. Teaching and school-based research requires one to become aware of, and avoid perpetuating, the damaging effects of using language in a biased and politically controlling way. Research on SEN and inclusion inevitably involves dealing with the historical and political trails of language, perceptions and attitudes. Consider, for example, the alternative interpretations of 'special' as 'different', 'better', 'not as good', etc. . . . Writing with a critical view of the concept of SEN, Corbett (1996, p. 49) suggests that:

> . . . when the term 'special' is applied to disabled people, it emphasises their relative powerlessness rather than conferring them with honour and dignity.

It is hard to separate the language of SEN from the perceptions and attitudes which we assume it represents. Indeed, the influential Russian psychologist Vygotsky (1986) suggested that language is important as an influence on thinking, not just as a means of expression. Corbett makes clear the ways in which the language which is used to describe disabled people can reflect and exacerbate longstanding negative perceptions and fears, whether the use of stereotypical and biased terminology has become casual habit or a more systematic and deliberately discriminatory practice (even if masked as 'joking'). The current reclaiming of offensive labels about disability (e.g. 'cripples') compares to what has also happened with black and gay communities in the latter part of the twentieth century.

There are many sources of good advice and guidelines for carrying out educational research in an ethical way (see the relevant chapters of Barnes and Mercer 1997; Clough and Barton 1995a, 1998; Cohen and Manion 2000; Hitchcock and Hughes 1995; Lewis and Lindsay 2000; Simons and Usher 2000). School-based researchers need to be aware of research ethics from the start and take steps to gain appropriate permission for data collection and reporting. The British Educational Research Association guidelines for good practice in educational research writing (BERA 2000, p. 4–5) include the following points to bear in mind:

Researchers in a democratic society should expect certain freedoms, viz: the freedom to investigate and ask questions, the freedom to give and receive information, the freedom to express ideas and criticise the ideas of others, and the freedom to publish research findings. These freedoms are essentially subject to good practice arising from the ethics of respect for persons and respect for truth (i.e. academic integrity). The research ethic of respect for truth requires researchers, in reporting data on persons, to do so in ways which respect those persons as fellow human beings who have entitlements to dignity and privacy. The research ethic of respect for truth, or academic integrity, requires researchers to be scrupulous in avoiding distortion of evidence and weakly supported assertions in the reporting of findings. Where conflict between the two ethical statements leads writers to use fictional constructions, it is good practice to make clear that this is the case.

Methodological issues

In planning the methods and procedure for a school-based research project it is essential to acknowledge the general characteristics of educational research as multidisciplinary, multivariate and multilevel (Keeves and McKenzie 1999, p. 208–9). These characteristics undoubtedly make educational research more complicated than we might wish, but they have direct implications for the research design, methodology and analysis of a 'real world' project aiming to be genuinely useful in school.

The *multidisciplinary* aspects of educational research have already been discussed in professional terms. In research terms one of the main challenges here is to relate educational principles and terminology to social, psychological and medical understandings of pupils with SEN. This applies even at the most basic level of deciding who and what the research is actually about (see Research tip 2.6).

Research tip 2.6 Incorporating psychological and medical terminology into educational research and practice: identifying the participants

In reading other people's research reports and disseminating one's own findings it is important to be clear about how the pupils involved were selected and defined (e.g. as 'dyslexic'), in order to understand the study and to decide if the results may be generalised to other children and young people in other contexts. Furthermore, teachers hoping to learn from and apply medical and psychological research on developmental differences between children need to address the implications in educational terms (this is often a problem in making use of information gathered about SEN 'conditions' e.g. from the internet).

In practice, good teaching can be identical for pupils with different labels or diagnoses, and pupils with similar diagnoses (e.g. Down's Syndrome) may benefit from rather different types of intervention. The diagnosis and label does not in itself allow conclusions to be drawn about day-to-day teaching and learning. However, categories can help with the communication and generalisation of research findings when the definitions are clearly drawn and everyone understands them in a similar way.

The categorisation of pupils is controversial and it arouses strong feelings, especially when it draws attention to certain characteristics and behaviours over others. Research problems arise in the attempt to communicate concerns, questions, intentions and findings when the language is imprecise. So 'dyslexia', for example, may be a highly technical term describing the test responses of a small group of pupils with certain neurological strengths and weaknesses, or it could be used more broadly in educational settings to describe a rather larger group of pupils who have specific reading and spelling difficulties in school. Terms such as 'dyslexia' or 'autism' are 'compressed' (Bayliss 1998, p. 69–70) in that they include a range of assumptions which have to be teased out in research using a variety of methods in combination (see Research tip 2.7, and Chapter 4).

Research tip 2.7 The language and definitions of SEN, and the relevance of people's perceptions and attitudes

Research on SEN and inclusion inevitably comes up against the ways in which people's differing beliefs, attitudes and perceptions are embodied in the language and definitions of SEN and inclusion. An effective response to problems of communication, bias and different interpretations is to gather data from different sources and check the findings against each other ('triangulation'). This might mean:

- using different methods to investigate the same topic (e.g. interview, questionnaire and observation);

- varying the level of questioning or observation (e.g. comparing general beliefs about dyslexia with specific instances);
- using systematic methods for defining relevant information (e.g. adopting specific behavioural descriptions to explain broad terms such as 'difficult');
- discussing the different interpretations of terms like 'off-task', including the pupil's perceptions and experience compared to his/her observable behaviour;
- involving different people in interpreting the findings and attempting to reconcile alternative perceptions and views;
- explicitly presenting controversial views and alternative interpretations to prompt discussion as part of the research process.

The limitations of simple categorisation arise because of the *multivariate* character of education and educational research. Teaching and learning for individuals and groups of pupils involve complex relationships between many variables operating simultaneously, including those relating to the pupils, teachers, curriculum, school and community settings. So this calls for the use of research methods which can cope with many variables, such as case studies, action research (however 'messy', Cook 1998) or multivariate statistical techniques (see Chapter 4). Furthermore, the *multilevel* aspect of educational research requires recognition of how the relevant variables operate and interact at different levels and contexts in education, from the individual pupils, peer groups and homes, to the class, school and broader sociocultural and political setting. Acceptance of this point is central to planning an effective research project, and later on in this chapter we will introduce a multilevel model which we use as the basis for the research framework presented in Chapter 4.

There are clearly significant methodological issues for research into SEN and inclusion. In his discussion of research in special education, Schindele (1985, p. 8) summarises the special conditions which create demands for any researchers investigating 'real life' problems in this area and which affect research decisions and strategies. These conditions include:

1. the 'special' population, with its diversity between and among groups of pupils – which can make it difficult to identify sufficiently large and representative groups of research participants;
2. the 'special' environment, with its range and diversity of teaching approaches, treatments, institutional settings and professionals – which affects the generalisability of research findings between different contexts;
3. the 'special' education process itself, with its dynamic, complex, multi-dimensional and individualised nature – which affects the validity of the research if interacting variables are not fully taken into account.

For these reasons, much SEN research raises specific issues about measurement and data collection, particularly with regard to problems of reliability and validity in the use of traditional experimental designs and statistical techniques. Relevant factors include the lack of appropriately norm-referenced measures; the need to adapt tests and procedures to specific disabilities and individual differences; the multiplicity of teaching programmes in use, often individualised; and the need (as Schindele argues) to focus as much on interpretations and processes as on outcomes of teaching and learning, using qualitative approaches. Schindele (p. 9) also remarks on specific ethical and moral considerations in that any decision about special treatments may have a significant – positive or negative – effect for pupils with SEN: '. . . because of their small number and their dependence on specialist provision they risk being misused by research'. Schindele's general conclusions are that SEN research needs to be interdisciplinary, it must investigate change over time and must be ambitiously complex in gathering qualitative and quantitative data which can get at the meaning of people's experience and involve them actively in this process:

> . . . such research must not only describe facts but also strive to understand subjective definitions and complex relationships; discovering meanings is as important as evaluating quantitative facts. (p. 6)

This chimes with more recent writing which takes an interpretive or critical perspective. At issue here is the validity of the knowledge and understanding which is produced by research. As Clough and Barton (1995b, p. 3) argue:

> . . . research itself creates – rather than merely studies – the phenomenon of special education/disability, and hence the constructs which researchers themselves bring to the work are important determinants not only of the success of the study itself but indeed also of the nature and direction of the field itself.

To work in an appropriately complex way with an understanding of the underlying assumptions, there is a need to see beyond the broad research paradigms discussed in Chapter 1. Dyson (1998) has suggested that it is possible for researchers following different traditions to have a dialogue rather than a confrontational dispute. Indeed, as Evers (1999) argues, we might best see educational research as intrinsically 'coherent', given the purposeful and inventive ways that people learn to solve practical problems:

> . . . some inclusive account of the structure of substantial theories needs to be given, especially one able to deal in a less brittle way with the graded, limited and context dependent nature of social science generalizations . . . . (S)ince much research in education concerns **practices**, some way of formulating practical knowledge needs to be found. (p. 271)

Teachers are usually experts in this respect.

Moving towards researchable questions

School-based research in the areas of SEN and inclusion may benefit from several different perspectives, as we have seen above. However, we have to start somewhere, and an individual study will be most effective and manageable when it focuses – initially at least – on the level of analysis which relates most closely to the purpose which the teacher has in mind. For example, concerns about the progress of a particular individual or group of pupils with reading difficulties may lead first to the evaluation of a class-based reading programme over the course of one term while alternatively, concerns about the number of pupils in school who have relatively low or uneven scores in the National Tests could prompt a year-long systematic investigation of the overall literacy policy and practice in school. As we will see in Chapter 4, clarity about the *purpose* of a school-based research project is central to planning an effective and useful investigation at the appropriate level of analysis.

The focus on *school-based* research in the area of SEN reflects the significance of understanding the social and educational context of pupils' learning and behaviour when defining SEN, understanding inclusion and deciding on teaching strategies. Children grow and learn in different contexts and there are no simple ways to investigate the whole picture, but there are some potentially useful models which can provide a framework for investigation and analysis. In considering how to investigate the interactions between children and their learning environments, Bronfenbrenner (1992, p. 193–4) writes about the value of identifying *ecological niches* – i.e. the 'particular regions in the environment that are especially favorable or unfavorable to the development of individuals with particular personal characteristics'. Bronfenbrenner's *ecological* model of child development (adapted in Figure 2.2) draws attention to the significance of interactions between children and:

- the immediate contexts of their behaviour, social interaction and learning (e.g. the classroom, playground or home);
- the relationship between two or more contexts in which they participate and learn (e.g. home and school links);
- the wider contexts in which they do not participate directly but which have an indirect influence on their development and education (e.g. teachers' Continuing Professional Development (CPD) courses; parents' employment; other children's friendship groups);
- the underlying structural and cultural features of the society, subcultures and organisations in which they are growing up (e.g. cultural values and beliefs; economic processes; local and national policies on education; organisational systems).

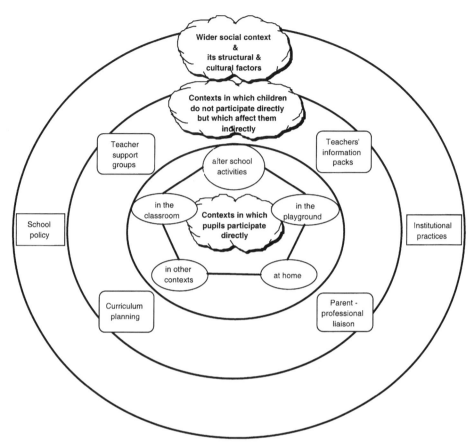

Figure 2.2 The contexts of children's development and learning (adapted from Bronfenbrenner 1992)

Understanding SEN and inclusion requires a model of at least this complexity (Sontag 1996; Howie 1999), and large scale studies might be expected to approach the topic on two or more of Bronfenbrenner's levels. For example, Evans (2000, p. 71) comments on the fact that discussions about inclusion tend to focus on humanitarian and equity concerns, whereas he argues that 'funding' and 'standards' are more significant issues in the broader context of educational reform. So in researching inclusion, Evans suggests that evidence about the allocation of funding, the costs of inclusive and special schooling, and the impact on standards achieved with *all* pupils, needs to be added to the more familiar investigations of school organisation and management, curriculum development, classroom organisation, support systems, parental and community involvement, and training. Smaller scale school-based research projects may be equally ambitious in working at different levels (e.g. a 'reading difficulties' study which includes classroom observation, examination of home–school reading diaries and an investigation of teachers' knowledge and understanding of literacy), but a 'modular' approach can be equally valuable when it involves the accumulation of individual self-contained and manageable projects which focus on gathering data in one context at one level of the system. Small-scale projects can be extremely successful and useful in their own right and raise questions for further research. They can also make a valuable contribution to a larger scale project in different settings (See Research tip 2.8). The point is that research which at least acknowledges these different contexts of activity and change has the best potential to map onto teachers' similarly wide-ranging interests, activities and responsibilities in different settings.

Research tip 2.8 Different levels of analysis: the value of collaboration

Teachers' school-based research may appropriately focus on gathering evidence about the wider educational context and the structural and cultural features of the educational system as well as the immediate processes of day-to-day teaching and learning. However, this need not be an individual task. Collaborative research by teachers in different contexts (schools, LEAs, countries) can be particularly effective for investigating structural/cultural factors.

In Chapter 4 we show how it is possible to develop school-based research focusing on pupils' experience and interactions in different contexts, adults' experience and interactions which have direct and indirect influences on pupils, and structural features of the contexts of learning and teaching. The challenge for school-based research is to formulate well-focused research questions at the relevant level(s). For example, at the 'pupil' level, initial research questions may be directed towards understanding learning and behaviour in different contexts, using exploratory questions at the start (see Research tip 2.9).

Research tip 2.9 Exploratory questions about pupils' learning and behaviour in different contexts

Awareness of the significance of the context in which learning and behaviour takes place raises a fundamental question in research. Consider, for example, a research project focusing on pupils with behavioural difficulties: to what extent is the 'difficult behaviour' merely a representation of a pupil's reaction to that specific environment as opposed to a more generic and persistent pattern? For pupils with SEN this is a crucial consideration in research on the assessment and intervention process. For example:

- Are difficulties observed in a number of different environments or just one setting?
- How does the pupil perceive the demands and expectations in each setting?
- How do the pupil's difficulties change certain aspects of each setting, including other people's behaviour?
- What are the pupil's beliefs and feelings about their behaviour?

If anti-social behaviour is observed only in school then might it be important to investigate other contexts as well? Further, if a pupil is assessed in one context (his/her own home or local school, for instance) and then an intervention takes place in another context (e.g. a children's home or special class), will what is achieved in the second context be transferable?

Such questions attempt to take account of the influence of the contextual factors from the pupil's point of view, and the influence of the pupil on the contexts of development (see also Chapter 1).

The questions about pupils' experience and interactions in different settings outlined in Research tip 2.9 can be linked to questions focusing on adults' responses and decision making, and associated structural factors and processes. This helps to connect the identification of problems with the development of strategies for solving them. There are a number of different exploratory and decision-making questions which might be asked. Does the research project aim to shed light on:

what is happening?
why/how it is happening?
what happens if/when . . . ?
is it effective for the intended purpose?
is it 'right' in relation to values and moral judgement?

These questions are aimed towards the description, analysis and evaluation of previous or current experiences, or of interventions carried out as part of the research. The focus may be on individuals or groups of pupils or adults in different contexts, depending on the purpose of the research project. The topic of interest is central to the investigation, and an early strategy in planning a research project can be simply to map out the decisions which have to be made in order to begin to see what the options are. These decisions include consideration of the extent to which a teacher is prepared to change the organisation of the classroom context and relationships (e.g. pupil grouping) and the degree of intervention (e.g. introducing a new teaching strategy) for the purposes of research (Freeman 1998, p. 23). See Figure 2.3 for an example relating to the topic of reading difficulties.

One of the main tasks of school-based research is to formulate research questions which will allow the research to actually begin. In Table 2.1 we give some examples of research questions which may arise from current interests and knowledge about the topic in hand – in this case an interest in pupils' reading difficulties.

Research questions guide the 'research visit' which is made to people in their different contexts of learning and teaching in the form of interviews, observations, questionnaires, etc., so it is important to be specific about the main research interests and priorities. When planning the actual methods and procedures to be

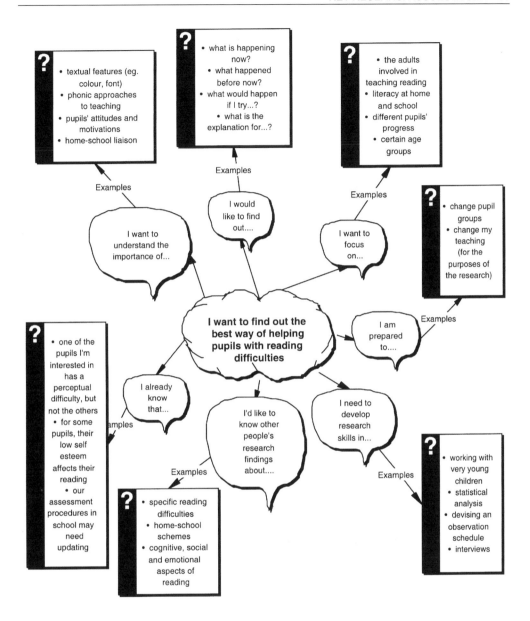

Figure 2.3 Mapping out your interests and decisions

used in a research project, the questions in Table 2.1 would need to be made more precise by identifying key factors such as the participants, the contexts and time scale. For example, the question 'How do pupils' attainments in reading compare with progress in other subjects?' could be refined to 'How does the progress of Year 1 higher and lower attainers in reading compare to their progress in maths over a period of one term, under ordinary classroom teaching conditions?'

Table 2.1 What do you want to find out about pupils' reading difficulties?

'I want to find out . . .'	What is happening?	Why/how is it happening?	Is it effective and just?
	DESCRIPTION	ANALYSIS	EVALUATION
Previous experience	What opportunities did pupils have for reading at home before starting school?	What are the connections between different types of pre-school reading opportunities and pupils' current reading difficulties?	How well do parents prepare their children for learning to read?
Current experience	How do pupils' attainments in reading compare with progress in other subject areas?	What factors seem to explain discrepancies in pupils' reading compared to other subjects?	To what extent do different subjects in the school curriculum allow the inclusion of pupils with reading difficulties? Is this sufficient?
The processes and outcomes of an intervention	How much use is being made of a new peer tutoring system designed to support pupils with reading difficulties?	Which aspects of the introduction of a peer tutoring system have most effect on teachers' and pupils' attitudes towards reading?	Does the introduction of a peer tutoring system improve pupils' attainment in reading? What are the advantages and disadvantages for the different pupils involved and for the school as a whole?

Yet as soon as the participants and contexts are defined (as has to be done), we come up against inherent limitations of doing so. If we use 'social addresses' or 'personal attributes' (to use Bronfenbrenner's (1992, p. 1 193) terms), such as gender, class, type of school, IQ score, etc., then only certain types of questions can be answered – usually with quantitative data. Alternatively, a 'person-context' approach in which we seek entry to the lived experience of teaching and learning in different settings such as the classroom or special unit, opens up new areas of investigation about the realities of provision for pupils with SEN – usually with qualitative data.

Focusing *only* on people's relationships and understandings, however, without identifying potentially relevant social addresses and personal attributes can result in missing important patterns and social processes (e.g. race/gender factors in SEN). Both approaches may be useful, as long as the advantages and limitations of each are understood in relation to the research questions. Both approaches may also be descriptive, analytic or critically evaluative, with all their associated assumptions. Table 2.2 provides some examples of the types of questions which can be asked when people and contexts are described from the 'outside' or the 'inside'. The rows indicate the connections between the ways in which pupils, adults and structural features of the contexts of learning and teaching are to be described, and the types of research questions which may then be asked (and vice versa). Reading down the columns would extend the possibilities. Further details of how this works in practice when planning and carrying out research are given in Chapters 3 and 4.

Table 2.2 Possible research questions for your 'research visit'

The research visit	Who? *(pupils/adults)*	Where? *(contexts of learning and teaching)*	Possible research interests and questions
Looking in from the outside **'Social addresses' and 'personal attributes'** **Likely to use quantitative methods**	gender, race, class, age, qualifications, test scores, medical syndrome, family position, home language, professional identity, etc. . . .	type of school, local environment, school policies, schemes of work, teaching programmes, assessment procedures, physical features of buildings, management structure, home–school communications, etc. . . .	• Does the introduction of a peer tutoring sytem improve pupils' reading test scores? • How often do primary class teachers meet fathers of pupils with SEN? • What types of secondary schools use integrated learning systems for pupils with learning difficulties? • Is there a disproportionate association between race, gender and pupil exclusions for behaviour? • How does the appointment of SENCOs to the senior management team relate to factors of gender, qualifications and years of teaching experience? • Does attendance at a staff development session run by the learning support department affect the number of requests for assistance from different subject teachers?
Seeking entry to the inside **'Person-context' interactions and processes** **Likely to use qualitative methods**	views, beliefs, preferences, self-concept, interpersonal communication, knowledge, friendships, behaviour patterns, coping strategies, professional practices, etc. . . .	social relationships, value dilemmas, classroom culture, professional collaboration, 'hidden' curriculum, teaching and differentiaton strategies, etc. . . .	• Which aspects of the introduction of a peer tutoring system have most effect on teachers' and pupils' attitudes towards reading? • How confidently do pupils with specific difficulties in reading and spelling view their progress across the curriculum? • How do pupils with behaviour difficulties cope with the conflicting demands of school and peer group? • How does a teacher's research into the nature of Down's Syndrome affect her/his classroom practice? • How are head teachers' perceptions of external pressures (e.g. school league tables) affecting decisions about pupil recruitment and allocation of teaching resources to pupils with SEN?

CHAPTER 3

Navigating published research on SEN and inclusion

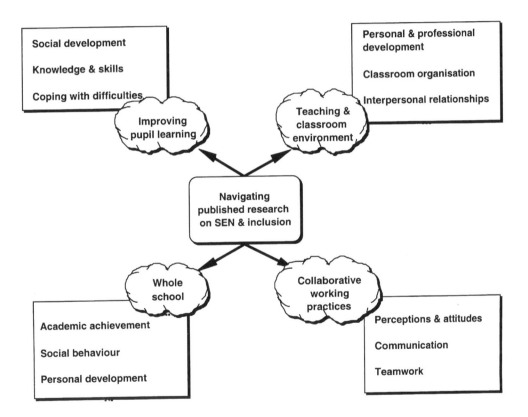

Figure 3.1 Outline of Chapter 3

At the end of Chapter 2 we discussed how to move towards 'researchable questions' about SEN. This is usually the beginning of a long journey. Any investigation will be subject to a good deal of selection, refining and reinterpretation along the way, sometimes to the extent of ending up with quite a different question from the one identified at the start. The aim of this chapter is to give an impression of the wide range of research in this area by offering a selection of studies which represent a variety of routes taken by researchers who have published their findings. Some were written by academic researchers based in universities or research organisations, and some by teachers combining research and teaching in their own schools (although it is still relatively hard to find published accounts written by practising teachers).

The four broad research questions which structure this chapter were chosen as examples of the topics which may interest a teacher researcher if the aims are to improve teaching and learning in school (Figure 3.1):

- How can we help pupils to learn more successfully in school?
- How can we improve teaching and the classroom environment?
- How can we develop collaborative working practices with other adults?
- How can the whole school be developed to respond to pupils' individual needs?

These interlinked research questions reflect the levels of analysis discussed at the end of Chapter 2, focusing in different ways on pupils' experiences and interactions in different contexts, on the experiences and interactions of adults who are involved in pupils' education, and on the structural features of the contexts of learning and teaching. They are connected to each other, and can be seen as different layers of interest (see Figure 3.2). They provide alternative starting points for individual research projects which may range from small-scale investigations of current practice in one classroom to large-scale analyses of whole-school procedures. In Chapter 4 we give examples of how school-based research questions may be approached at these different levels, depending on the researcher's specific purposes, interests and previous research experience.

We do not attempt to present a thorough review of research on SEN and inclusion. We have instead taken different aspects of the above questions and outlined typical topics of interest and methodological approaches. We then add summaries of some published research examples which were chosen eclectically to give an idea of the range of possibilities, and which help to show where individual research projects may fit into the 'big picture'. These research examples can best be seen as 'trail markers', which not only stand up in their own right, but also provide access to the wider field of research of which they are a part. Researchers build on each other's work, and the references included in a published article acknowledge these sources. So reading even 2–3 relatively recent articles can usually give quite a good impression of the other work that has been done in the area (this is discussed further in Chapter 5). Our suggestions for further reading included at the end of this chapter are intended to back this up, and for simplicity these take the place of references in the main text.

As discussed in Chapter 2, the rationale for carrying out research will influence the approach adopted, and certain questions can only be answered by adopting

Figure 3.2 Layered research questions for school-based research

particular approaches. So in reading and evaluating published research we need to have a sense of *fitness for purpose*. Does the methodology used by the researcher enable the collection of enough of the right sort of data to describe what is happening and to analyse the processes and relationships in accordance with the specific research questions? Is there enough information about the researcher's underlying intentions and assumptions to justify any evaluations and judgements that are made? What were the limitations of the selected methods, and is this made explicit in the research report?

The published examples given in this chapter can only offer a limited taste of the whole research process, which has already been interpreted and selected in order to produce the written account. There is no substitute for reading the original article or chapter, but access to journals and different styles of writing can make this difficult. So we have tried to include a range of sources in the hope (inspired by Goldilocks!) that if one does not fit with your current interests and another is too hard to find, then you will still find a reference that is 'just right' (or at least leads you in the right direction).

How can we help pupils to learn more successfully in school?

This question lies at the heart of most school-based research projects about SEN. Concerns about the progress of individuals and groups of pupils are what drives teachers to investigate the situation, to understand the factors which are contributing to learning and behaviour problems and to use the pedagogical knowledge and skills which will improve pupils' chances. The keys to promoting pupils' learning may actually be found in the wider educational context, as suggested by the other broad research questions covered in this chapter. However, in many cases the most productive and motivating research questions for teachers' investigations are directly linked to the pupils who are in some way being hindered in or excluded from learning in school.

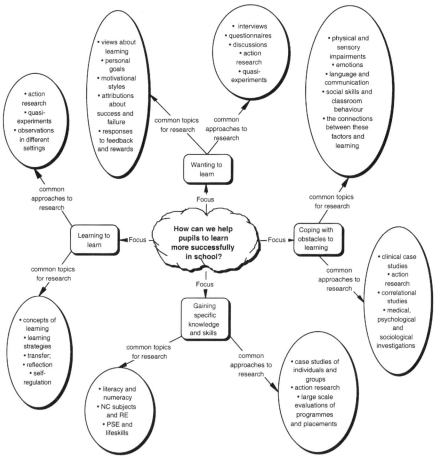

Figure 3.3 Pupils' learning: common research topics and approaches

Figure 3.3 shows some of the topics and approaches which commonly arise in thinking about how to help pupils learn more successfully. Research studies focus in different ways on pupils' learning and motivation, and on the various medical, psychological and social factors which might hinder pupils' progress in school.

It is, perhaps, inevitable that a high proportion of studies about pupil learning focus on literacy, given the emphasis of the school curriculum. However, there are also some very productive investigations of pupils' learning in the other subjects of the National Curriculum and RE, personal and social education and lifeskills for children with more severe and complex needs. One of the key research issues here is how to assess pupils' experiences, knowledge and understanding in a way that goes beyond descriptions of observable behaviour. Research attention has also been given to the reflective notion of learning to learn, which has been recognised as a important aim for pupils experiencing difficulty in learning school. The awareness and control of learning (metacognition) involves the appropriate use of learning strategies, the transfer of knowledge and skills to different subjects and contexts, and the processes of self-regulation which influence motivation and social behaviour as well as learning. Alternative motivations (e.g. peer approval vs. teacher praise) can prove to be an obstacle to learning in school, and many studies seek to understand pupils' feelings and attitudes in order to promote better engagement in learning. Researchers also focus in different ways on what to do about other apparent obstacles to pupils' learning in school – focusing, for example, on factors such as physical and sensory impairments, emotions, medical conditions, language development, social skills and classroom behaviour.

As outlined in Figure 3.3, several different approaches and methods are used for research on pupils' learning and motivation, including case studies of individuals and groups of pupils, action research, large-scale evaluations of programmes and placements, quasi-experiments, observations in different settings, interviews, questionnaires and discussions (see Chapter 4 and recommended readings for further information about research methods). Researchers may decide to gather both qualitative and quantitative data about the processes and outcomes of pupils' learning over a period of time. They may try out and evaluate a new intervention, carry out a survey of pupils' views about learning, or investigate the links between physical, social or emotional factors and learning processes and outcomes (using correlational studies or interventions). There will commonly be contact with pupils during a study, although in some cases researchers will analyse information (secondary data) that has been collected by other people for another purpose (e.g. teacher assessments). There will usually be some reference to the contexts of pupils' learning, varying in the detail and attention given. This is where we can look for connections between the studies which focus primarily on pupils' experience and progress, and those which ask questions about teaching and the classroom environment, collaborative working with other adults, and the values, policies and strategies underpinning whole-school development – as discussed later in the chapter.

Selected examples of research into pupils' learning

Only one source is given for each piece of research, although many studies can be found in several places, published for different audiences. Full references are given at the end of this chapter.

- Focus: understanding and responding to the experiences of 'quiet children' at primary/secondary transition (Collins 1996)
  Published in a book: *The Quiet Child*

Collins was concerned about the quiet withdrawn pupils in class who rarely spoke and seemed reluctant to ask for help. She argues that this might be seen as one type of SEN. Collins wanted to discover the causes of quiet behaviour, including the pupils' perceptions of their experience. She carried out 12 case studies of pupils, using semi-structured interviews over a period of three years during primary/secondary transition. She also interviewed parents and teachers, and carried out classroom observations. One of her main findings was that quiet pupils are not a homogeneous group (and not exclusively girls, as they are often perceived), although there are some common anxieties and frustrations among them. For example, from her observations she identified four different types of withdrawn behaviour and she looked at different strategies for enabling pupils to participate in class. Collins then presents further qualitative evidence about her experiences of devising, implementing and evaluating teaching strategies for quiet pupils, in both withdrawal groups and whole-class teaching.

- Focus: enhancing the science attainment and self-esteem of Year 8 students with learning difficulties (Dunsmore 1998)
  Published in a journal: *Improving Schools*

Dunsmore started his research project in the context of concerns in school about students' academic performance and attendance records. After discussing the evidence about links between academic achievement and self concept, he describes his work with a bottom set Year 8 class, with learning difficulties, focusing on the use of rewards to improve self-esteem and attitudes to science, strategies to improve peer collaboration and talk, and strategies to improve understanding of science through discussion of learning. Qualitative and quantitative data included test scores, diaries, classroom videos and interviews. He found a clear improvement on science test scores, but a more erratic response on the self-esteem questionnaire (perhaps, as he comments, due to the limitations of the questionnaire).

Qualitative evidence showed a large improvement in class participation, evidence of scientific understanding, positive attitudes and cooperation between students. Similarly positive results were found when the project was extended to other classes in school.

- Focus: helping secondary school boys with 'anger management' through groupwork (Dwivedi and Gupta 2000)
  Published in a journal: *Support for Learning*

Dwivedi and Gupta set their study in the context of the recognised limitations of certain behavioural techniques which do not enable students with emotional and behavioural difficulties to develop self management. They set up a school-based programme aiming to help Year 9 students to develop skills to cope with difficult situations, such as those which provoke anger and anxiety. This was in the context of a whole-school behaviour policy already in existence. The ten-week programme for 15 students involved discussion, role-play, relaxation exercises, assertiveness skills, 'thought directing', and problem-solving. Dwivedi and Gupta gathered evidence through staff discussion as the programme continued and via student 'Lost-it' logs recording incidents of 'losing your cool'. Students were also invited to comment on the usefulness of the group programme. The results showed a generally positive response from the students, with some qualifications about personal preferences and needs in a programme of this type. The student logs showed a quantitative increase in appropriately 'cooler' responses to difficult situations. Dwivedi and Gupta comment on the obvious gains from the programme, at least in the short term, although they recognise that it would have been appropriate also to gather evidence from school logs about students' involvement in difficult incidents.

- Focus: helping an apparently reluctant reader (Holland 1994)
  Published in a book chapter: *Action Research, Special Needs and School Development* edited by G. H. Bell *et al.*

Holland carried out a case study of a Year 2 child, S, whose progress in reading did not reflect the other more advanced knowledge and skills which she demonstrated in class (i.e. in talking, writing, painting, use of memory, etc.). Concerns had already been expressed by S's previous teacher, and a learning support programme had been put in place. Holland identified problems in S's attitude to reading, including some apparent anxieties. Holland consulted a teachers' action research network and gained advice and suggestions which led to an action research programme involving paired reading, the implementation of new approaches for writing and spelling and parental involvement in the classroom. Test scores showed improvement over a period of time beyond the intervention period. There was also qualitative evidence about S's improved attitude to reading and writing – to the extent of her asking to read aloud in class. Holland's study raises issues about the need to be alert to the many variables which can affect pupils' progress in a real classroom situation, and the value of sharing problems with 'outsiders' as part of the action research process.

- Focus: helping autistic children to engage in pretend play (Sherratt 1999)
  Published on the internet: Teacher Training Agency website

Sherratt wanted to investigate whether early years pupils with autism and additional learning difficulties can learn to use pretend play within a class group. He focused on eight 5–6-year-old pupils to take part in an intervention programme which included exaggerated, dramatic adult modelling of play scenarios (imaginative stories and constructions). Videos of these sessions were shown to the children, drawing out the most important aspects for them. Observations showed that the children's pretend and social play increased after the teaching programme, whereas this would not have been predicted from an assessment of their SEN beforehand. This challenges the traditional view of autism as a condition in which children are incapable of pretending and understanding other people's point of view.

How can we improve teaching and the classroom environment?

While much of the emphasis within SEN research is placed on how pupils learn, of at least equal importance is the consideration of what we teach, how we teach it and how best to organise the learning environment to facilitate pupil learning and effective teacher coping. Teaching and learning are inextricably linked – one might argue that you are only teaching when pupils are learning – but the focus in this section will be on the former. One of the main reasons for asking research questions about teaching and the classroom environment is the recognition that pupils' 'special educational needs' are in part created by the teaching they receive in different contexts. Pupils with even the most severe difficulties react differently in different settings. Teachers know this, and take steps to do something about the teaching strategies within their control, even if they cannot control the many factors which influence pupils outside of the classroom. In this way, an acknowledgement of certain pupils' 'special' educational needs may merge with teachers' responses to the individual needs of every school pupil. The classroom is itself a complex social setting – a fact which has drawn the attention of educational researchers for many years. So it is not surprising that there is already a wealth of research about teaching and the classroom environment, much of which has direct relevance to children with SEN.

Figure 3.4 shows some of the topics and approaches which commonly arise in thinking about how to improve teaching and the classroom environment. Research studies focus in different ways on approaches to teaching, classroom organisation, teacher–pupil relationships and teachers' own knowledge, skills and coping strategies.

Much of the research on teaching and the classroom environment focuses on teachers' knowledge, decision making and feelings. So studies of differentiation and classroom organisation do not just look at the repertoire of possibilities but also at the processes by which teachers come to use one approach over another in an increasingly complex and stressful professional role. The creativity of considering what might be possible in the classroom is shown in the evidence about how

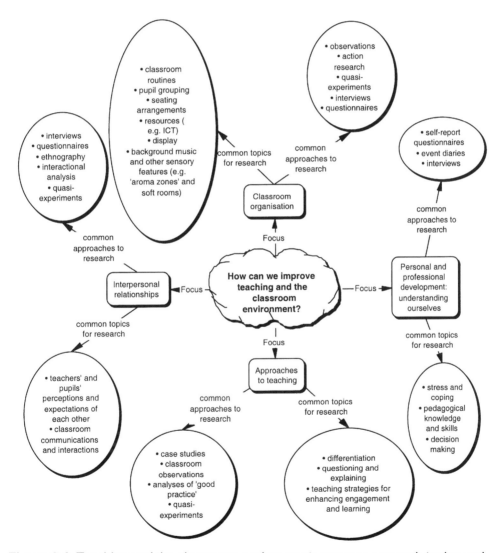

Figure 3.4 Teaching and the classroom environment: common research topics and approaches

teachers adapt their strategies in response to the pupils' needs, and to the demands of the school curriculum and organisation. Studies have looked variously at teaching materials, grouping strategies, furniture arrangements, background music, ICT, etc., and the implications for pupils' social behaviour, engagement and learning. Many investigations focus on the core curriculum subjects of English, mathematics and science, but there is also work across other areas of the curriculum – particularly in seeing how success in one area can increase understanding, motivation and self-esteem elsewhere. The dilemmas which arise in managing teaching strategies and classroom organisation are acknowledged in research about teachers' personal beliefs, stress and coping strategies. Researchers have also looked closely at the communications and interpersonal relationships between teacher and pupils, which not only help pupils to learn, but also maintain motivation and manage the classroom behaviour of the whole-class group. Typical areas of interest here include teachers' and pupils' perceptions and expectations of each other and the ongoing interactive processes in the classroom.

As outlined in Figure 3.4, several different approaches and methods are used for research on teaching strategies and the classroom environment, including case studies of individuals and groups of pupils, reports and analyses of 'good practice', action research, quasi-experiments, naturalistic observations, interactional analysis, ethnography, event diaries, interviews, questionnaires and discussions (see Chapter 4 and recommended readings for further information about research methods). Researchers may decide to report on current practice, e.g. methods they have used to introduce or develop particular topics such as history, or they might evaluate the introduction of a new initiative. Quasi-experimental methods offer the possibility of measuring pupils' progress using different methods of teaching and differentiation. Teachers' thinking and coping strategies may be investigated with self-report questionnaires which are analysed using sophisticated statistical techniques which weigh up different factors, or through the use of event diaries and interviews which are analysed using qualitative methods such as content analysis. Studies which collect data about the views of teachers and pupils offer the possibility of seeing the degree of match (or mismatch) and the mutual influences over a period of time. They link neatly into the studies of pupils' learning discussed in the previous section.

Selected examples of research on teaching and the classroom environment

Only one source is given for each piece of research, although many studies can be found in several places, published for different audiences. Full references are given at the end of this chapter.

- Focus: organising the layout of primary classrooms to enhance inclusion (Lucas and Thomas 2000)
  Published in a book chapter: *Putting Research into Practice in Primary Teaching and Learning*, edited by S. Clipson-Boyles

Lucas and Thomas set their study in the context of a growing understanding of the value of seeking pupils' views when attempting to create more inclusive learning environments. They present reports of two small-scale classroom research projects: one with 10–11-year-olds, focusing on observed differences in the pupils' on-task behaviour when sitting individually and groups; the second describing a study in which a teacher changed the classroom layout, giving a clear rationale for her actions to her 9–10-year-old pupils and involving them setting class rules for behaviour. The second study proved to have positive effects on participation and pupil behaviour, including a noticeable effect on the social inclusion of a pupil with SEN rejoining her own class. The authors conclude that these case studies, together with other research findings in the area, 'show that significant changes can be made in the way the classroom is organised to cater for special educational needs, and indeed the needs of all children in the class' (p. 32).

- Focus: comparing primary teachers' strategies for more able mathematicians (Allebone 1998)
  Published in a journal: *Education 3–13*

Allebone carried out comparative case studies with Year 5 classes in two schools, focusing on pupils identified by the teachers as more able mathematicians. The research involved videoed observations of maths lessons over a period of six weeks, aiming to analyse the teaching approaches (especially the organisation of whole-class teaching and groupwork) and the ways in which the teachers' questions potentially extended the pupils' thinking skills. Using Bloom's taxonomy to analyse the teachers' questions in terms of cognitive demand, Allebone found that with certain types of organisation, teachers asked a higher proportion of cognitively demanding questions (as when working with small groups of pupils with similar ability compared to whole-class teaching). Allebone comments that teachers' use of different teaching styles reflects broader educational aims as reflected in the curriculum (e.g. more diversity or more homogeneity?) – an important point bearing in mind the international comparisons made between pupils' maths attainment.

- Focus: investigating a reception class teacher's use of educational theory as a tool for developing inclusion (Alton-Lee *et al.* 2000)
  Published in a journal: *International Journal of Inclusive Education*

Alton-Lee *et al.* present a detailed account of case studies carried out in New Zealand, focusing on the responses of one teacher, Ms Nikora, to a course where she learned about two theoretical models of disability: 'social constructionist' and 'personal tragedy'. Social constructionist models see disability as a product of social factors, while personal tragedy models have their origins in medical perceptions of individual deficits or pathology. The case studies involve collaborative action research carried out in the context of a larger project on pupil learning in a multicultural primary school. Data was collected from video observations, interviews, and pupils' work samples. Transcript extracts are provided to tell the stories of certain classroom incidents, and the research is written up as an extensive 'interrupted narrative', in which the reader is asked at several points to reflect on what she or he might do in similar circumstances. One of the main findings is that Ms Nikora used 'multiple positionings' in a social constructionist understanding of individual pupils with SEN (e.g. seeing both their similarities to other pupils and their individuality). This is discussed in terms of the limitations of the 'personal tragedy' model of disability.

- Focus: stress and job satisfaction: a study of English primary school teachers (Chaplain, 1995).
  Published in a journal: *Educational Psychology*

Chaplain examined the relationship between stress and job satisfaction among a sample of around 300 primary teachers using a self-report questionnaire, generated from earlier research into teachers' accounts of their experience of stressful events. Teachers were asked to rate 18 aspects of teaching (such as 'motivating pupils to learn') in terms of how stressful they found each item and how frequently these items prove stressful. He compared groups of teachers in terms of sex, age and teaching experience. Data were analysed using principal components analysis – (a statistical method of reducing a large number of correlated variables to a smaller number of underlying factors). Three 'stress' factors were identified and labelled: Professional concerns; Pupil behaviour and attitude and Professional tasks. The first stress factor, Professional concerns, included items concerned with supporting pupils with SEN and achieving personal goals. In contrast, teachers gained most satisfaction from their perceived performance as teachers, which was related to positive feedback from children. On the basis of this study, Chaplain produced a model to demonstrate the relationship between the stress factors and specific facets of job satisfaction.

- Focus: using information and communications technology (ICT) to optimise the sensory environment for pupils with visual and other sensory impairments (Tobin 1996)
  Published in a book: *Learning Through Interaction: Technology and children with Multiple Disabilities*, edited by N. Bozic and H. Murdoch

Tobin uses case examples to illustrate the ways in which ICT can 'optimise' the physical environment to help pupils with sensory impairments. He refers, for example, to a 6-year-old pupil, Nicoll, with profound hearing loss, very limited vision and low muscle tone. The aims were to increase Nicoll's attention span and to see if he could control the computer using switches. Using a software program with clear, simple images, set up in a small bare room with no external light, it was found that Nicoll took control and was highly motivated to watch the screen for longer than his usual attention span. These observations and other case examples are discussed by Tobin as evidence about the interdependence of sensory modalities and the importance of understanding pupils' learning in context (rather than in terms of separate measurable skills). He comments on the need to train teachers appropriately and allow teachers to work with software designers to identify and extend the educational possibilities of ICT.

- Focus: setting up a 'Quiet Place' to help young children with emotional and behavioural difficulties in mainstream schools (Spalding, 2000)
  Published in a journal: *British Journal of Special Education*

Spalding writes about the use of the 'Quiet Place' to provide therapeutic support to young children with emotional and behavioural difficulties and their families. The Quiet Place is a room in school designed 'to promote a sense of peace and relaxation' (p.128), with soft furnishings, toys, plants, musical instruments, etc., which relate to a theme (e.g. fairy tales). Children attend for an agreed number of sessions per week, meeting relevant therapists. Spalding presents evidence about the effects of the Quiet Place for a sample of 22 children compared to a control group over a six week course. The data is gathered from standardised developmental profiles completed for each child, supplemented by interviews with parents and teachers. The experimental group showed progress compared to the control group, but not at a statistically significant level. Qualitative analysis of the interviews, however, showed some patterns which may explain individual children's progress. Extensive interview quotes illustrate different views about the workings and positive effects of the Quiet Place as a preventative, multidisciplinary intervention, particularly in socially deprived areas.

How can we develop collaborative working practices with other adults?

One of the most significant developments in recent years has been the attention given to the teacher's role in the multidisciplinary team responsible for identifying and responding to pupils' special educational needs and developing inclusion. Within school, much of this collaboration is focused on the relationship between teachers, SENCOs and learning support assistants (LSAs). Beyond school, the SEN

Code of Practice (DfEE 2000b, p. 31) discusses the need for an integrated 'seamless' service involving healthcare professionals, social services departments, specialist LEA support services, and other providers of support services including voluntary agencies, to work in partnership with pupils teachers and parents (see also Chapter 1).

The question of how to develop collaborative working practices with other adults has attracted a lot of research interest – unsurprisingly, given the potential problems discussed in Chapter 1. It is a challenging field of school-based research due to the professional issues arising in carrying out investigations which involve professional colleagues and parents. It inevitably involves reflecting on one's own practice and professional relationships. Figure 3.5 shows some of the topics and approaches which commonly arise in thinking about how to develop collaborative working practices with other adults. Research studies focus in different ways on the processes of communication, collaboration and multidisciplinary decision making, on innovatory practices in teamwork and on the perceptions, knowledge and attitudes of the participants.

Parental involvement in education was innovatory in its time, and this field of research has been extended to look at various forms of home–school partnerships, at support services and more recent efforts to move towards 'joined-up' working (especially in the early years, in certain special education contexts, and for school leavers). The processes involved in working together have been of interest to researchers, often focusing on what happens in specific contexts and procedures such as case conferences and the use of individual education plans (IEPs) by different school staff. A lot of this research has been informed by investigations of the views of all involved and the languages in which these are expressed. We know that different professionals and parents are likely to have different beliefs and goals, even if the shared aims are to improve the educational opportunities and outcomes for children with SEN. So studies of people's perceptions and opinions about SEN and inclusion, their understandings of different roles, expectations and intended outcomes, can be particularly useful for gaining insight into collaboration and making it work better.

As outlined in Figure 3.5, several different approaches and methods are used for research on collaborative working practices with other adults, including action research, case studies, reports and analyses of 'good practice', observations in different settings, interviews, questionnaires, discussions, discourse analysis and document analysis (see Chapter 4 and recommended readings for further information about research methods). Researchers may use interviews and questionnaires with different groups of professionals and parents to see the degree of match in belief and opinion. They may trace the development of new initiatives, often as participant observers. They may model decision making procedures and look for hierarchies of power and status in teams. The research in this area links closely to studies of teaching and the classroom environment in looking at how

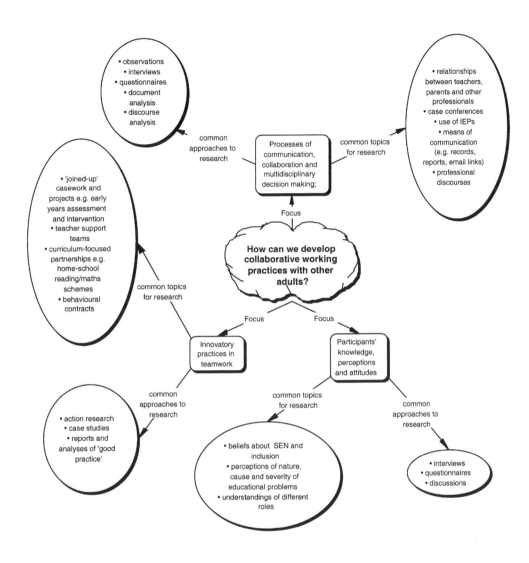

Figure 3.5 Collaborative teamwork: common research topics and approaches

teachers work with other adults in the classroom. There are also strong connections to investigations of the whole school in seeing how values, procedures and practical arrangements (such as the availability of a telephone during the day) may hinder or help teachers to work effectively with other adults in and out of school.

Selected examples of research into collaboration between adults

Only one source is given for each piece of research, although many studies can be found in several places, published for different audiences. Full references are given at the end of this chapter.

- Focus: comparing the views held by different agencies about the nature of 'successful education' for 'looked after' children in foster care (Coulling 2000)
  Published in a journal: *Support for Learning*

Coulling sets this study in the context of current moves towards inclusion and the assocated multi-agency working. She carried out structured interviews with 25 individuals, including teachers, social workers, home-finding officers, foster carers, and children in foster care. She sought to elicit each person's 'personal constructs' (see Chapter 4), by prompting the adults to identify and compare successful and unsuccessful children, and by asking the children to reflect on how their teachers had perceived them. The key indicators of success were identified as sociability, attendance and 'reaching potential', all influenced by the quality of foster care and the school's ability to understand the needs of children in foster care and liaise with the foster carer. She found that the different professionals and children had similar aims and understandings about successful education, particularly in the importance of helping children in foster care to socialise and make friends in school.

- Focus: comparing the beliefs about learning difficulties held by staff in a secondary school (Skidmore 1999b)
  Published in a journal: *British Educational Research Journal*

Skidmore wanted to investigate the relationship between the provision of learning support within the school and the teachers' views about how to respond to pupils with difficulties. He carried out semi-structured interviews with a range of staff in different management positions. He also analysed relevant documents, including the school's SEN policy. He gave feedback to the school staff and incorporated the subsequent discussion into the analysis of the data. He found two main discourses of learning difficulty in use – that of 'curriculum presentation' (i.e. planning, differentiation, learning and teaching strategies, etc.), and that of 'pupil ability' (i.e. the abilities, needs and weaknesses of individual pupils). He uses his findings to challenge the traditional view that 'healthy' and effective organisations require consensus among staff. Instead he claims that 'staff subscribing to divergent discourses of learning difficulty may be able to negotiate a working agreement in support of a specific practical initiative' (p. 660), giving a new reading support programme as an example. However, he speculates that the divergent opinions may be more significant for the school's development in the longer term.

- Focus: 'Joined-up' working in the early years (Dodd and Saltmarsh 2000)
  Published in a journal: *Special Children*

Dodd and Saltmarsh describe the development of a multidisciplinary service, involving the education and health services. The services had been housed together previously but had only developed *ad hoc* liaison, sometimes overlapping in their responsibilities. They developed a protocol to aid the services in working together more effectively with young children and their families, and they present two case studies which show the range of professionals involved with each family and links between them. From their professional experience they summarise the advantages and disadvantages of collaboration between services, and in general terms they relate their report of 'good practice' to the growing research evidence about the value of multidisciplinary approaches.

- Focus: understanding practitioners' views about the practical value of nurture groups in mainstream infant schools (Cooper and Lovey 1999)
  Published in journal: *European Journal of Special Needs Education*

After discussing the philosophy and development of nurture groups, Cooper and Lovey present the results of a questionnaire survey given to 35 delegates to a conference on the topic. The participants included teachers, head teachers, educational psychologists, a nurse-therapist, a consultant psychiatrist and a DfEE representative. They asked people about the distinctive nature of support offered by nurture groups, about the children who would benefit from this provision and about how the school is affected by having a nurture group. They summarise the conclusions, which were generally positive, and give extensive illustrative quotes relating to the potential emotional, social and educational benefits for children. They note some disagreement about certain aspects – particularly regarding people's views about the causes of children's emotional and behavioural difficulties. In describing children who would benefit from a nurture group, some focus on the effects of pre-school experience, others on current difficulties. As they comment, this could be significant given the potential problems in apportioning 'blame' for children's SEN to early experience within the family.

- Focus: using classroom support in a primary school (Rose 2000)
  Published in a journal: *British Journal of Special Education*

Rose was interested in the relationship between teachers and learning support assistants, particularly in the issues arising about where support should be directed (e.g. individual child or whole class) and how it should be organised. He carried out his case study in a large junior school (Key Stage 2), with a high proportion of pupils with SEN and a commitment to developing an inclusive school ethos. He carried out semi-structured interviews with 10 teachers and observed a sample of 6 pupils in the classroom for a full school day each. In presenting the findings he focuses on the role of learning support assistants (LSAs). The teachers saw LSAs as 'as a critical factor in enabling the sample pupils to be included in classroom activities' (p. 193), remarking on their contribution to all aspects of teaching. Every class had at least one full-time assistant, but the observations showed considerable differences in the degree of one-to-one support given to individual pupils. Rose interprets this as showing the value of flexibility and giving LSAs responsibilitiy to decide how long to spend with individuals, depending on the activities and groupings at the time (e.g. whole-class teaching, groupwork, etc.) and on pupils' individual needs. Although cautious about generalising from one case example, he suggests some principles for employing LSAs to support effectively within the whole class and work in collaboration with teachers on planning, teaching and evaluation.

How can the whole school be developed to respond to children's individual needs?

This question captures recent debates about the nature of SEN and how best to respond to pupils' educational needs. Primary, secondary and special school teachers all work with groups of individual pupils, and both teachers and pupils have their own experiences, hopes, strengths and weaknesses in relation to the aims and procedures of the school environment. We saw earlier in this chapter that research on pupils' learning can be effective and rewarding. Yet research on pupils' learning, on teaching strategies and the classroom environment and on collaborative working with other adults can only be understood in the whole-school context. This leads some researchers to address their efforts at the whole-school level and ask their first research questions about the values, curriculum, management structures, routines and school ethos which influence pupils' learning and behaviour.

Figure 3.6 shows some of the topics and approaches which commonly arise in thinking about how to develop the whole school to respond to pupils' individual needs. Unsurprisingly, it is complex, given the range of factors which may contribute. Research studies focus in different ways on the school as a system (including policies, organisation, resources and staff development), curriculum and assessment, social relationships and links and influences beyond individual schools. The growing attention to incorporating pupils' views is also reflected at this level in the studies which make a direct link between encouraging pupils to express their ideas and using this information to improve the whole school.

Figure 3.6 can only give an impression of the wide range of research carried out at the whole-school level. Examining the school organisation and structures allows the researcher to look for patterns of activity (and bias) which may not be obvious at the individual pupil or classroom level. It also offers a way of seeing how different roles and practices fit together and interact over time. Research on curriculum and assessment often goes beyond seeking better ways to teach the set curriculum. Recent work has focused on extending and enriching the curriculum, sometimes using psychological models of individual differences as a guide (e.g. Gardner's (1993) theory of 'multiple intelligences'). Research on social relationships has also

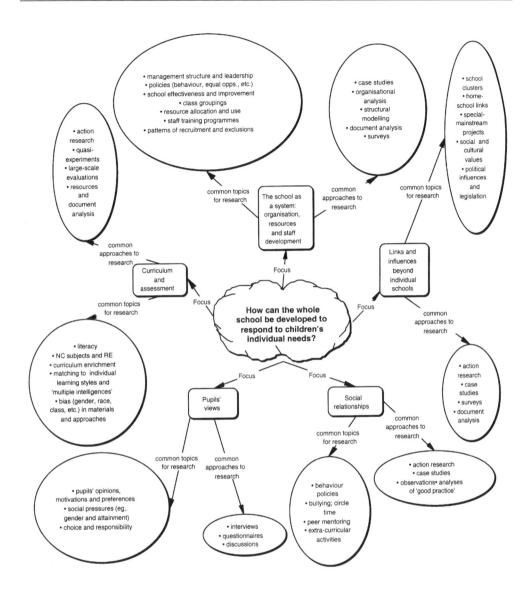

Figure 3.6 Whole-school development: common research topics and approaches

investigated innovations such as peer mentoring schemes (e.g. in reading), the prevention of bullying, and the impact of extra-curricular activities (e.g. adventure trips) on pupils' learning and motivation. Research on pupils' views and on links beyond the school have a connection in the attention they draw to factors which are outside teachers' direct control. The means of balancing pupils' needs and interests with political and social values and expectations, and making this work in school is a complex professional skill which calls loudly for research and dissimenation of good practice.

As outlined in Figure 3.6 several different approaches and methods are used for research on developing the whole school, including case studies, action research, surveys, document analysis, systematic and ethnographic observations, reports and analysis of 'good practice', interviews, questionnaires, discussions, quasi-experiments, large-scale evaluations of programmes and placements, organisational analysis, and multi-level modelling (which allows the simultaneous measurement of different variables and relationships at different hierarchical levels – including pupils, teachers, classes and whole school) (see Chapter 4 and recommended readings for further information about research methods). Researchers may decide to introduce a new programme or strategy and evaluate its success in quantitative and qualitative terms. This can be particularly powerful when links are made to other schools trying similar initiatives in their own contexts. Ethnographic research calls for immersion in school culture, identifying the key features, relationships and cultural tools which allow the school organisation to work (e.g. rules and procedures, and the language in which shared views are expressed). School documents can be important sources of data, as can statistical evidence (e.g. examination results). Interviews and discussions (e.g. to seek pupils' views) may be incorporated into school practice, in this way demonstrating how research and teaching may become inseparable.

Selected examples of research into whole-school development

Only one source is given for each piece of research, although many studies can be found in several places, published for different audiences. Full references are given at the end of this chapter.

- Focus: monitoring to raise attainment and investigate underachievement in a secondary school (Hanks 1998)
  Published in a book: *Teacher Research and School Improvement*, edited by R. Halsall

Hanks was concerned about apparent underachievement of pupils at GCSE, and about her own success in monitoring the work of pupils and teachers in her faculty. She used action research to tackle these problems, hoping as she went along to involve the teachers actively. She set up a system of collaborative monitoring, using examples of pupils' work from different subjects. Most of the research was carried out in regular faculty meetings, supplemented by questionnaires completed by her Year 10 tutor group. Hanks describes the progress of her research over a series of four meetings. She soon found that no clear pattern emerged to explain underachievement in terms of individual differences between pupils (e.g. self-esteem). However, she identified certain categories which emerged about pupils' work habits and then discussed these with the pupils involved. As a result of her research new monitoring procedures were introduced in school, systems were set up to share good practice, and Hanks reported to colleagues and governors. Hanks reflects that '(w)hile improvement may be relatively easy to achieve in the short term, it needs to be sustained over a period of time for any change to be proved to be effective' (p. 177). However, she comments on the particular value to the staff team of having established a supportive climate in which problems could be tackled collaboratively.

- Focus: dealing with bullying in special school (Torrance 2000)
  Published in a journal: *British Journal of Special Education*

After reviewing the extensive literature about the factors influencing bullying in school and the potential consequences for pupils, Torrance sets out to fill what she sees as a gap in qualitative research in this area. She presents a case study of bullying in a special school for pupils with social, emotional and behavioural difficulties, addressing research questions about the existence of bullying in this context and the interventions which might be effective to prevent bullying. She used both quantitative and qualitative methods, including document analysis, questionnaires, observations, interviews and sociometric analysis, to gain insight into the relationships and social interactions in the school (even as a whole and certain specific locations such as the tuck shop queues. This variety of methods was designed to allow the cross-checking of data from different sources ('triangulation'). Her findings indicated that bullying *did* exist in this small school with high teacher-pupil supervision) and that certain patterns emerged which distinguished bullying in this context from mainstream findings. Torrance comments on the sensitivity of her research (e.g. regarding staff responses to the findings), and she argues for the need to carry out qualitative case studies in particular school contexts if research on bullying is to have a positive effect on practice.

- Focus: introducing Feuerstein's Instrumental Enrichment in a school for children with social, emotional and behavioural difficulties (Head and O'Neill 1999)
  Published in a journal: *Support for Learning*

Head and O'Neill were concerned about the limited short-term gains of the strategies currently in place to improve pupils' academic achievement and behaviour, so they decided to introduce a 'thinking skills' programme to promote the longer-term generalisation of learning to new and unfamiliar situations. The school management team decided to pilot Feuerstein's Instrumental Enrichment (IE) programme with a group of six pupils, while retaining a control of pupils with similar abilities and emotional and behavioural problems. They ran the programme for 20 weeks, with four lessons a week, and evaluated it through teacher observation of the lessons, a pre- and post-course questionnaire for the teachers, and a discussion involving the whole-school staff. Head and O'Neill present qualitative and quantitative findings about changes in academic performance, cognitive functioning and behaviour of the IE group compared to the control group. They also describe the differences between pupils with individual profiles of progress. In conclusion, they comment positively on the value of the IE programme in their experience, noting that it requires commitment from staff and pupils and cannot be seen as a quick, 'magical cure'.

- Focus: listening to pupils in secondary schools (Griffiths 1996)
  Published in a book: *Listening to Children in Education* edited by R. Davie and D. Galloway

Griffiths describes a series of initiatives designed to improve the ways in which pupils express their views and are listened to in school. Initially, classroom observations focused on communication between teachers and pupils, and as a result of this, active tutorial work was given priority in the timetable. After establishing a whole-school plan for providing opportunities to listen to pupils, Griffiths explains the structural changes they made in response, including changes to the class groupings and the pastoral system. Staff development became central to this process, and a number of staff embarked on courses which included research projects addressing topics relevant to communication with pupils. Griffiths describes the various benefits which accrued over several years, including improved examination results and fewer exclusions. This account of 'good practice' is then discussed in terms of the structural features of secondary schools and the external pressures (e.g. league tables) which can affect the development of a 'listening school' (p. 88).

- Focus: developing a secondary school's response to pupils' individual needs (Buckle *et al.* 1999)
  Published in a journal: *Special Children*

Buckle *et al.* provide an account of one aspect of the work of a secondary school which is working to meet all its students' individual needs. This includes a systematic monitoring of student performance from Key Stage 2 test results onwards. They present quantitative data to illustrate the effects on reading test scores of a reading programme introduced to specific students in Year 9 after assessments at the start of the year. They describe the relevant contextual factors, including the resource allocation, programme activities and liaison with parents and students. They also present some qualitative evidence about the positive student responses. This account of 'good practice' is extended with reference to further school programmes for literacy support, student mentoring, curriculum enrichment for particularly able students and in-class support by older students. They comment on how all the changes put into place require 'hard-headed prioritising of time' (p. 12), and that this in itself has implications for seeing the SEN provision as a resource for the whole school rather than individual students.

References for the research examples summarised in this chapter

Allebone, B. (1998) 'Providing for able children in the primary classroom', *Education 3–13* March Issue, 64–69.

Alton-Lee, A. *et al.* (2000) 'Inclusive practice within the lived cultures of school communities: research case studies in teaching, learning and inclusion', *International Journal of Inclusive Education* 4 (3), 179–210.

Buckle, L. *et al.* (1999) 'Every need is special', *Special Children* 117, February, 9–12.

Chaplain, R., (1995a) 'Stress and job satisfaction: a study of English primary teachers', *Educational Psychology* 15 (4), 473–489.

Collins, J. (1996) *The Quiet Child.* London: Cassell.

Cooper, P. and Lovey, J. (1999) 'Early intervention in emotional and behavioural difficulties: the role of Nurture Groups', *European Journal of Special Needs Education* 14 (2), 122–131.

Coulling, N. (2000) 'Definitions of successful education for the "looked after" child: a multi-agency perspective', *Support for Learning* 15 (1), 30–35.

Dodd, L. and Saltmarsh, L. (2000) 'Joined-up working', *Special Children*, 127, March, 24–27.

Dunsmore, A. (1998) 'Improving science attainment and student self-esteem', *Improving Schools* 1 (2), 54–58.

Dwivedi, K. and Gupta, A. (2000) "Keeping cool": anger management through group work', *Support for Learning* 15 (2), 76–81.

Griffiths, T. (1996) 'Teachers and pupils listening to each other', in R. Davie and D. Galloway (eds) *Listening to Children in Education*, 77–89. London: David Fulton Publishers.

Hanks, K. (1998) 'Monitoring students' work to raise attainment and investigate the problem of underachievement', in R. Halsall (ed.) *Teacher Research and School Improvement: Opening doors from the inside*, 167–178. Buckingham: Open University Press.

Head, G. and O'Neill, W. (1999) 'Introducing Feuerstein's Instrumental Enrichment in a school for children with social, emotional and behavioural difficulties', *Support for Learning* 14 (3), 122–128.

Holland, J, (1994) 'An apparently reluctant reader', in G. H. Bell *et al.* (eds) *Action Research, Special Needs and School Development*, 113–118. London: David Fulton Publishers.

Lucas, D. and Thomas, G. (2000) 'Organising classrooms to promote learning for all children: two pieces of action research', in S. Clipson-Boyles (ed.) *Putting*

Research into Practice in Primary Teaching and Learning, 25–36. London: David Fulton Publishers.

Rose, R. (2000) 'Using classroom support in a primary school: a single school case study', *British Journal of Special Education* **27** (4), 191–196.

Sherratt, D. (1999) 'Teaching children with autism to use pretend play', in Teacher Training Agency: *Teacher Research Grant Projects 1998*, http://www.canteach.gov.uk/info/research/grant/summaries98_99.htm

Skidmore, D. (1999b) 'Divergent discourses of learning difficulty', *British Educational Research Journal* **25** (5), 651–663.

Spalding, B. (2000) 'The contribution of "Quiet Place" to early intervention strategies for children with emotional and behavioural difficulties in mainstream schools', *British Journal of Special Education* **27** (3), 129–134.

Tobin, M. (1996) 'Optimising the use of sensory information', in N. Bozic and H. Murdoch (eds) *Learning Through Interaction: Technology and children with multiple disabilities*, 56–65. London: David Fulton Publishers.

Torrance, D. A. (2000) 'Qualitative studies into bullying within special schools', *British Journal of Special Education* **27** (1), 16–21.

Further reading

(including individual studies and reviews of research – some with an international perspective)

Alderson, P. and Goodey, C. (1998) *Enabling Education: Experiences in special and ordinary schools*, London: Tufnell Press.

Bell, G. H. *et al.* (eds) (1994) *Action Research, Special Needs and School Development*. London: David Fulton Publishers.

Chaplain, R. (2000) 'Educating children with behaviour difficulties', in D. Whitebread (ed.) *The Psychology of Teaching and Learning in the Primary School*, 300–322. London: RoutledgeFalmer.

Croll, P. and Moses, D. (2000) *Special Needs in the Primary School: One in five?*, London: Cassell.

Hornby, G. *et al.* (1997) *Controversial Issues in Special Education*, London: David Fulton Publishers.

International Special Education Congress (ISEC) (2000) *'Including the Excluded'*, held at the University of Manchester, 24–28 July 2000. Conference papers published on CD-ROM, available from Inclusive Technology (http://www.inclusive.co.uk).

Kershner, R. (2000) 'Teaching children whose progress in learning is causing concern', in D. Whitebread (ed.) *The Psychology of Teaching and Learning in the Primary School*, 277–299. London: RoutledgeFalmer.

Lewis, A. and Norwich, B. (1999) 'Mapping a pedagogy for special educational needs', BERA (British Educational Research Association) National Event Report, *Research Intelligence* **69**, 6–8.

Pijl, S. J. *et al.* (eds.) (1997) *Inclusive Education: A global agenda*, London: Routledge.

Rose, R. and Grosvenor, I. (2001) *Doing Research in Special Education*, London: David Fulton Publishers.

Rudduck, J. *et al.* (eds) (1996) *School Improvement: What can pupils tell us?* London: David Fulton Publishers.

Speece, D. L. and Keogh, B. K. (eds.) (1996) *Research on Classroom Ecologies: Implications for inclusion of children with learning disabilities*, Mahwah, NJ: Lawrence Erlbaum Associates.

Vulliamy, G. and Webb, R. (eds) (1992) *Teacher Research and Special Educational Needs*, London: David Fulton Publishers.

Watson, J. (1996) *Reflection Through Interaction: The classroom experiences of pupils with learning difficulties*, London: Falmer Press.

CHAPTER 4

Ideas into action: the research process

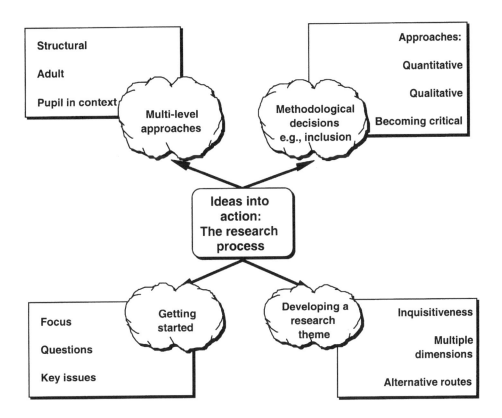

Figure 4.1 Outline of Chapter 4

In this chapter we look at how to carry out a research project and in doing so incorporate a number of the issues raised in the previous chapters. This chapter addresses four areas (Figure 4.1):

- Multilevel approaches to answering research questions – structural, adult and pupil in context;
- Examples of different foci and research questions concerned with key issues in SEN research;
- A comparison of ways to research *inclusion* using three different research approaches;
- Developing a research theme.

Table 4.1 A Framework for Research on SEN

Level of analysis	Possible focus	Potential research questions	Process
Structural Social policy – Community – LEA – School	The organisation and effectiveness of inclusion policies in school	How is inclusion managed in this school?	Object
	Funding policy for SEN pupils and those without SEN	On what basis does the LEA transfer funds to individual schools? How is this money used to support pupils with SEN?	Method
	Local community support agencies and organisations for SEN	Which parents do local voluntary groups support?	Outcome
	National information and advice on inclusion	To what extent is the NFGL Inclusion website informed by and responsive to teachers in different phases and sectors of education?	
Teachers and carers Inter group – interpersonal – individuals	Teachers' and carers' perspectives on inclusion	To what extent do teachers and carers share common perspectives on inclusion?	Object
	Teachers' and carers' representations of pupils' academic potential	Do the expectations of teachers and carers match in retrospect of pupil performance?	Method
	Parent–professional liaison	What procedures are necessary to establish effective learning support?	Outcome
	Teachers contribution to statementing procedures	How might teachers increase their knowledge of specific types of SEN or syndromes and how might the specific knowledge differ from general knowledge about SEN and inclusion?	
Pupils Intergroup – interpersonal – individual	The learning experiences of 'included' pupils with SEN	How do the experiences of pupils with sensory impairments (SI) in special and mainstream schools compare?	Object
	Pupils' coping styles	What strategies do pupils with reading difficulties adopt in order to cope with school?	Method
	Social relationships among groups of pupils with SEN	What does friendship mean to pupils with EBD?	Outcome
	Contrasting the affects of different group structures on learning	What effect does group size have on the learning experiences of shy pupils?	

Alternative ways of answering the question		
Quantitative	**Qualitative**	**Becoming criticial (quantitative and/or qualitative)**
Measuring effectiveness of different ways of organising inclusion	Case study of how inclusion policy is managed in a single school	Establishing level of resource available for pupils with SEN and other groups
Contrast value added between KS3 and KS4 in several schools with similar number of pupils with SEN	Identify – legislative requirements and guidance + school policy + staff/pupils' + parents' + managers' perspectives. Observation	Record quantity, quality and value of resources available. Ask pupils and teachers about ease of access and perceived availability
Collect KS3 and KS4 results and use *multiple regression* to test predictive power of different forms of organisation on KS4 outcomes	Review secondary data, official literature and school documents. Interviews with SMT, teachers, parents and pupils	Review official literature + costing of resources from official sources + interviews + attitude scales
Measurement of teachers' and carers' beliefs about inclusion	Study the quality of relationships between teachers, SMT and parents of pupils with SEN	Examination of the status of SEN by comparing the salary and career prospects of SEN teachers with those of subject teachers
Questionnaire and attitude scales (Likert Scale)	Personal constructs analysis (Repertory grid technique)	Collect secondary data on salaries (interviews and chart career histories)
Analyse relationship between different groups: build model to represent relationships using ANOVA	Generate personal constructs for teachers and parents and use this as a basis for exploring the degree to which they share common understanding and where differences exist	Compare data on salary structures and career paths of SEN teachers with subject teachers. Interview teachers and parents to obtain personal perspectives on status of SEN
Measure the effects of teaching pupils how to analyse problem structures on their ability to solve problems	Track pupils with SI through their school week; observe and ask them to indicate where they feel most and least supported	Compare the quality of teacher–pupil interaction in mainstream and special schools
Quasi-experimental approach	Event-focued study	Observation and recording Flanders Interaction Analysis + photo/video analysis
Select two groups of pupils with SI; pre-test skills, teach and measure changes in performance. Use a third group as a control	Observe and record pupils during lessons and social activity at predetermined times during the school play. Supplement through interviews with pupils to gain their perspective on what happened and how they felt about it. Build model of pupil perspective alongside own observations	Measure teacher and pupil interaction and determine in what ways the quality of relationships differ in the two locations

Multilevel approaches to answering research questions

The cornerstone of this chapter is Table 4.1 which provides the reader with an overview of alternative ways one might approach research into key issues relating to SEN at three different levels: structural; adult and pupil in context. To annotate the table we will offer examples of the types of questions you might ask at each of these different levels and how you might engage with the same question using three different research approaches. We do not wish to suggest that what we offer is a comprehensive treatment of *all* possible approaches, but we aim to give the reader some insight into contrasting and complementary ways of engaging with a research question.

Table 4.1 is divided into seven columns, the first three of which identify possible areas for study and levels of research activity. The remaining four columns look in more detail at how a project on inclusion might be approached at each of the three levels (pupil, adult and structural) and using three different descriptive and analytic approaches (quantitative, qualitative and becoming critical).

The first column identifies three different but related levels of analysis, namely:

- *Pupil level* the direct experiences of pupils in different contexts – for example, learning, social behaviour, relationships with peers;
- *Teacher and carer level* activities among teachers and carers which have an indirect effect on pupils' personal experiences – for example, learning support, teacher expectations, teacher development, collaboration with parents;
- *Structural level* at this level the concern is with the bigger picture – for example, national policies affecting SEN provision and management, community influences, school policies.

As we have discussed elsewhere in this book, using hierarchical levels of analysis as a frame of reference is not to suggest that these three levels are mutually exclusive. They do however, serve to highlight the potential benefit to a researcher of determining a particular level at which one might begin to engage with a problem and identify an appropriate methodology. So, for instance, while a connection could be demonstrated between a pupil learning and changes to social policy, it may not be appropriate to be drawn into a debate about the social justice of such a policy, if you are merely interested in how a pupil solves a particular type of problem in maths. This does not mean to say that you should ignore other influential issues, but in order to make a project manageable one has to impose some constraints or boundaries.

Being conscious of the different levels is also helpful in deciding both the range of possibilities for investigation, as well as identifying potential difficulties in accessing data. Furthermore, it is also not uncommon to move between levels in order to pursue the answer to a particular question – so while in your initial project might look at developing say, an SEN policy in your school, subsequent projects may adopt a 'top down approach'. This might involve examining how the policy translates into practice for teachers and carers and/or pupils. We will come back to this issue later in this chapter.

Examples of different foci and research questions concerned with key issues in SEN research

In the second column of Table 4.1, a range of different foci for each of the three levels is offered to illustrate the types of issues you may wish to tackle in your particular project. The lists offered are not exhaustive but provide a sample range of possibilities – you will no doubt think of many more!

At each level of analysis in Table 4.1 the first 'focus' is separated from the rest and expanded to highlight how to set about developing a research question (in our example about inclusion) suggesting what you might look at, which method to use, and how to analyse and interpret the results. To show how different researchers might engage with the 'same' question the final three columns demonstrate contrasting ways of answering the 'same' question.

The third column offers possible research questions which you might choose to ask within each area. Again the first question in each of the three blocks is developed further.

Column four offers levels of activity within a project, moving from setting objectives through suggesting a method to offering a likely intended outcome for the research.

The final three columns demonstrate how each of the sample questions could be approached using the three different perspectives namely, quantitative, qualitative and critical (where both quantitative and/or qualitative methodologies might be used). In other words the 'same' question is approached in different ways. It is to a brief discussion of the content of these three columns that we now turn.

A comparison of ways to research inclusion using three different research approaches at three different levels of analysis

Example 4.1	
Level:	Structural
Focus:	The organisation and effectiveness of inclusion policies in school
Research question:	How is inclusion managed in this school?

Quantitative approach

The first approach suggested is quantitative, which inevitably involves the numerical analysis of data *but those of you who hate maths don't switch off!!* Most of the calculations involved can be done quite easily on computers or even calculators. There are also a number of good and easy to read books on different statistical methods available.

The quantitative researcher might *operationalise* (define a concept or variable so that it can be measured or identified) the effectiveness of inclusion policies as: the measured performance against a common marker (say GCSE or KS3 test, for instance) in two (or more) schools who organise inclusion in different ways. In doing so the researcher is predicting (stating a *hypothesis*) that different types of organisation may result in different levels of pupil performance (or no difference – a *null hypothesis*). Put another way, if a particular way of organising inclusion is effective then this effectiveness might be demonstrated in pupils making more academic progress. To make sure that one school doesn't have an advantage over another the pupils studied in each school are matched in terms of previous academic performance, social class, sex, etc. To determine whether or not the differences between two schools are not just the result of chance (bias in the sample) statistical tests are used to confirm the differences.

In the example given a method known as *multiple regression* is used. This technique provides an estimate of the effect of a predictor variable (e.g. the way in which inclusion is managed) on a single dependent variable (e.g. GCSE performance) while controlling for the effects of other variables (e.g. sex, previous academic performance or social class). In other words, you may find when 'eyeballing' the data that there seems to be more improvement in the GCSE performance of pupils with reading difficulties in one school than in another. On the surface this may appear to indicate that one approach is more effective than another. If however, you control for the effects of sex and previous performance you may find the difference is much less and may even be reversed. In other words the differences between the sexes is far greater than that between schools. Second, while the difference in the scores of the two schools may appear 'significantly' different it does not mean that these differences are *statistically significant.* To be statistically significant in most of the tests used in this type of research you should be able to demonstrate that the differences due to chance are no greater than $P < .05$ or five per cent (or even higher e.g. $P < .01$ that is, the chances of the differences being a fluke are 100:1). You will need to be aware of the mathematical assumptions that are made when using such tests, *for example* the size of your sample and the level of measurement, and these must be determined *before* collecting the data.

Further reading
Dunbar, G. (1998) *Data Analysis for Psychology*, New York: Arnold. (Chapter 5)

Qualitative approach

In contrast to the above quantitative approach a researcher adopting a qualitative approach is more interested in words than in numbers. Although an oversimplification, the 'word–number' distinction serves to highlight a key difference between quantitative and qualitative approaches, that is, how the researcher perceives the world and how each treats the data collected (since both might use similar methods to collect the data).

In the 'structural level' example, a case study is suggested as an appropriate means of investigating inclusion. This approach necessitates an in-depth study of the strategies for inclusion in one particular school. In using this technique it is important that you are clear about the boundaries of the 'case'. While a 'school' may seem to infer a physical boundary (the school perimeter) many aspects of schooling take place outside the perimeter (sports for instance). Alternatively, the school day may be used as one boundary but again much decision-making, planning and administration takes place after school and, in many instances, in teachers' and head teachers' homes. While not wishing to create confusion, it is essential for you to identify the boundaries of your study in order to maintain your focus.

Here the emphasis is on detail and 'thick' description of relationships and processes in a natural setting – not an artificially constructed phenomenon created just for research purposes as in the case of an experiment, for instance. To provide such a level of description will inevitably require a combination of methods which might include the collection of official documents (including LEA guidance school policies as well as minutes from formal and informal meetings), interviews, questionnaires and observation (as a participant and/or non participant). Thus the researcher will make use of multiple sources to gain insight into the nature of the structure, processes and relationships of the case.

A case study then represents a research strategy and not just a method for collecting data. Given that the focus is on one particular school it is important to consider why that school (out of so many) has been selected. In selecting a particular school you should therefore justify your choice. Justifications for making a particular choice can include: availability (your own school for instance); official recognition (e.g. by OFSTED) as a 'good' example of inclusion practice; you have been asked to investigate what is happening and so on. Given that the emphasis is on depth (understanding a single case) as opposed to breadth (examining a number of schools) generalisation to other schools is problematic or 'fuzzy' (Bassey 1999).

Further reading

Cohen, L. and Manion, L. (2000*) Research Methods in Education*, 5th edn, London: Routledge. (Chapter 9)

Bassey, M. (1999) *Case Study Research in Educational Settings*, Buckingham: Open University

Critical approach

The central concern of this approach is to empower underprivileged groups and the approaches used can be either or both quantitative and qualitative. At the structural level one might be interested in seeing to what extent the rhetoric of LEA funding priorities translate into practice for pupils with SEN. In doing so the researcher will focus on collecting data from a range of sources including secondary data sources, such as literature searches of legislation and guidance relating to support for pupils with SEN and LEA documentation, such as budgets and financial allocations; school policy documents and resource allocation. In addition primary data might be collected through interview and questionnaires to ascertain the views and attitudes of key players such as governors, teachers, parents and pupils.

There are clearly benefits in collecting data from a range of sources and combining them so as to generate a more comprehensive picture of what is going on. This process of using multi-methods is often referred to as triangulation (see, Denzin 1970). The term is analogous with navigational triangulation where two or more coordinates are used to locate a particular position in space – in research terms this means using a number of different perspectives to allow a more complete picture of what is going on. Triangulation in research terms exists in many forms such as using a combination of methods (methodological triangulation) or carrying out research at different times (time triangulation).

However, it is important to note that using multi-methods requires the use of different analytical techniques, both quantitative and qualitative, in order to interpret the data, which raises issues in terms of how one might bring the analyses together. It is often the case that one methodology is more dominant than others so for instance, interviews are used to provide a 'thick' description of a particular situation and supplemented by larger questionnaire-based surveys or vice versa. Which method is most dominant often depends on individual preference or previous experience and where this is the case care should be taken to ensure you are familiar with both approaches rather than just 'throwing' an additional dimension into the equation.

Further reading

Cohen, L. and Manion, L. (2000) *Research Methods in Education*, 5th edn, London: Routledge.

Denzin, N. K. (1970) *The Research Act in Sociology: A theoretical introduction to sociological method,* London: Butterworth.

Example 4.2

Level:	Teachers and carers
Focus:	Teachers' and carers' perspectives on inclusion
Research question:	To what extent do teachers and carers share common perspectives on inclusion?

Quantitative approach

In answering this question the quantitative approach suggested is the measurement of people's attitudes – an area of measurement which is extensively used but is far from simple. Researchers often turn to either questionnaires or to attitude scales to determine people's views and use either existing examples or design their own. It is important that you recognise that there are a number of pitfalls in designing your own scale which relate to two important aspects of research design – validity and reliability. Put simply, validity is concerned with whether an instrument measures what it claims to measure, whereas reliability is concerned with whether your measure gets similar results when used more than once. There are a number of different forms of validity the simplest of which is face validity. A measure of this is gained by looking to see if the questions appear to be relevant to the research question, in other words, whether on the face of it the questions on your scale make sense. A common way of checking face validity is to ask someone knowledgeable in the field to take a look at your measure. Other forms of validity include: external validity – the degree to which your findings are relevant to contexts and subjects beyond those in your study; and construct validity – the degree to which your scale measures the constructs you are interested in (e.g. attitude) as they are generally understood.

When designing questionnaires and scales it is important to avoid ambiguity, something which is often easier to say than do – given the problems that professional questionnaire designers are faced with (note the fiasco in the USA presidential election (2000) where it was claimed that voters were confused when completing a voting slip specifically designed to make voting more simple!). One way of overcoming some of these difficulties is to pilot the instrument before using it in the research project. Piloting involves getting a sample of people to complete the scale and asking them afterwards to comment on the questions and what they feel they were being asked about. Furthermore, If you are planning to contrast the views of two distinct groups then you might wish to pilot scales to both groups and determine through analysis whether the scale does in fact discriminate between them before embarking on your main study.

In constructing your scale it is important to be aware of how you intend to analyse the results, which means paying attention to the level of measurement you will use. Phenomena can be measured at a number of levels each conveying differences between values. There are four levels of measurement, ranging in strength from nominal (the lowest level) through to ordinal, interval and ratio (the highest level). The nominal level is purely descriptive (e.g. male or female; married or unmarried) and while you may give the labels a number (e.g. male = 1 female = 2) you cannot use these numbers in calculations (e.g. adding a male (1) to a female (2) is meaningless). In contrast an ordinal measure (e.g. very happy, happy, not sure, unhappy, very unhappy) gives some impression of quantity. However, the distance between very happy and happy is not necessarily the same as between unhappy and very unhappy.

The next highest level of measurement is interval. Here the distance between each point on the scale is equal such as temperature in Fahrenheit (the distance between 10° and 15° is the same distance as between 60° below and 65° below.. Thus the scores from an interval scale can be added or subtracted. However, interval scales do not have an absolute zero.

Ratio scales are the highest level of measurement and because they have an absolute zero it is possible to make mathematical statements about the data. So in the case of height the distance between 155 cm and 160 cm is the same as that between 200 cm and 205 cm. Most importantly, someone who is 100 cm is exactly half the height of someone 200 cm high. (NB You can describe higher level data using lower level measures but not vice versa.)

Most attitude questionnaires and scales rely on ordinal level measures, such as the *Likert Scale,* where respondents indicate their level of agreement with a statement (e.g. strongly agree, agree, disagree, strongly disagree). There is considerable controversy among researchers as to what level of measurement must be used to enable you to use certain statistical tests with confidence, since they require certain assumptions to be made about the level of measurement and the distribution of scores. Your reading of the research literature in your chosen field will provide you with a guide as to what is considered the most appropriate level of measurement.

A third essential consideration before embarking on your study is how you plan to analyse the results. In the example provided the suggested method is analysis of variance (ANOVA) which is a test of the statistical significance of differences between two or more groups on one or more dependent variable(s). So one might wish to compare the attitudes towards inclusion (dependent variable) of SEN teachers, subject teachers and carers (independent variables) in one particular school. Attitude could be defined as the total score on your attitude scale (or a number of sub-scores). Within each group there will be a range of scores and it is likely that there will be some overlap – even if the mean (average) scores for each group seem very different. ANOVA determines whether the sum of the differences (distances from the mean) between the various groups is significantly greater than the sum of the differences within the groups by measuring the ratio between the two. If the variance within the groups is greater than that between the groups then the difference will not be significant. Don't forget that finding a significant difference is not the same as establishing why they differ: that's for you to interpret.

Further reading
Breakwell, G. *et al.* (1995) *Research Methods in Psychology*, London: Sage. (Chapters 4 and 12)
Dunbar, G. (1998) *Data Analysis for Psychology*, London: Arnold. (Chapter 4)

Qualitative approach

In the qualitative approach to the question the concern is with the quality of the relationships between teacher and carers. One way we can begin to understand the nature of interpersonal relationships between members of different groups, is to find out how individuals within those groups perceive each other, since how one individual perceives another influences their subsequent behaviour toward them, often unwittingly. However, asking people their opinions of others directly can mask what they really think, as they are likely to moderate their explanations to make them seem socially acceptable. To overcome this, 'masking' techniques have been developed to try and accurately determine people's true representations of their worlds. One technique used to explore individual representations comes from the psychology of personal constructs. This approach developed by Kelly (1955) argues that people act like scientists and develop their representations of their worlds so as to predict and control events. He also argued that an individual's representation of the world consists of a limited number of categories or constructs. These categories are bipolar so the construct is made up of two contrasting words (e.g. good–bad, kind–nasty). For Kelly, the only way to understand the individual is to discover how they construct their world. There are a number of ways of eliciting people's constructs ranging from listening to what they have to say to a technique known as the repertory test. This is not a single test and the technique can be varied to reflect the type of issue being investigated and who is being questioned.

In our example we might ask teachers and carers separately to identify a list of ten pupils, five of whom have SEN and five of whom do not. The names are then written separately on pieces of card. Each adult is presented with the cards (upside down) and asked to select three at random. Then ask each the following question

I would like you to tell me something about these three people. In what important way are two of them alike but different from the third?

Invariably the individual will produce a word to describe how two of the people are the same – this is called the emergent pole. They may then have to be asked again in order to produce the contrast (implicit pole). This is a difficult task and may take some time. It is essential that even during prolonged silence while the individual is searching for a word that you resist the temptation to offer one. You may however, help them to reduce a sentence or long phrase to a short one or single word. Having produced a list of constructs which should not exceed 40 (and may be a lot less, Kelly suggested that we tend to have seven or eight major constructs) the researcher may then ask questions to add further meaning to the list of words. Sometimes an apparently concrete term hides the true meaning – but don't be put off if constructs, which are important to you are not generated, as they may not be relevant to other people. The task of the researcher is then to interpret the various constructs and this can be done in a variety of ways (Fransella and Bannister 1977). The results are often depicted in the form of a grid which allows the easy comparison of clusters of constructs or people. It has been suggested that people are attracted to those who share similar constructs (Bannister and Fransella 1974) since agreement from others increases self-confidence, providing common ground for doing things together. The potential usefulness of this approach to those wishing to work together to include pupils with SEN becomes apparent.

Further reading
Bannister, D. and Fransella, F. (1974) *Inquiring Man: The psychology of personal constructs*, 3rd edn, London: Croom Helm.
Cohen, L. and Manion, L. (2000) *Research Methods in Education*, 5th edn, London: Routledge.
Fransella, F. and Bannister, D. (1977) *A Manual of the Repertory Grid Technique*, London: Academic Press.
Kelly, G.A . (1955) *The Psychology of Personal Constructs, Volumes 1 and 2*, New York: Norton.

Critical approach

Social groups within schools are organised hierarchically and these hierarchies are often linked to curriculum subjects. The status of teachers could be conceptualised in terms of their salaries, career prospects, involvement in decision making, access to training and availability of socially valued resources. While these variables do not capture all the ways in which one group differs from another they clearly represent one way of operationalising teacher status. From a critical standpoint, if we are to raise the status of pupils with SEN in the mainstream school then by implication we must ensure that those who teach them are perceived as having at least equal status with any other teacher. In engaging in this type of research one has to be aware that it is a potential minefield since professional status lies within the very thorny area of personal and social worth, salary, qualifications and professional competence. As with other areas of a similar ilk (teacher stress, behaviour management) some people may well be reluctant to discuss how they feel about the issues. The approach suggested in the example requires identifying salary structure along with charting career histories using interview. The latter is similar to producing a life history in that the researcher is interested in identifying how and why individuals ended up in a particular situation and allowing them the opportunity to extend and develop their explanations.

Further reading
Breakwell, G. *et al.* (1995) *Research Methods in Psychology*, London: Sage. (Chapter 21)

Example 4.3

Level:	Pupil
Focus:	The learning experiences of included pupils with SEN
Research question:	How do the learning experiences of pupils with sensory impairments in special schools compare with those placed in mainstream schools?

Quantitative approach

The focus in this example is upon the problem-solving-skills of pupils with sensory impairments who have undergone different teaching conditions (mainstream or special school). We have opted for a quasi-experimental study (see Fife-Schaw in Breakwell *et al.* 1995), so called because the researcher is able to manipulate some of the variables but cannot randomly assign subjects to experimental and control conditions. Unlike the previous examples, that were more 'naturalistic', in experimental conditions the researcher attempts to isolate a specific activity in order to measure the effects of a particular treatment (e.g. teaching package).

There are a number of ways in which we can measure problem-solving skills including social and practical competencies as well as intellectual ones. The researcher will obviously have his/her own agenda in this respect. To simplify our explanation we will show how one might evaluate the effects of teaching pupils how to analyse problem structures and the effects of this training on the problem-solving skills of pupils with sensory impairment. To do this the pupils first complete a test (pre-test) to determine their current level of competence in analysing problem structures and then undergo training after which they will again be tested (post-test). The performance gains for each group will be measured and then compared with each other. Our hypotheses might look like this:

- There will be no greater improvement in the ability of pupils to analyse problem structures as a result of training, and;
- There will be no differences in the performance of pupils with sensory impairments in special schools compared with those in mainstream schools.

These statements are referred to as null hypotheses, since they predict that there will be no differences resulting from any of the conditions. The evidence may then challenge this.

Our quasi-experiment will involve three groups of pupils: two groups with sensory impairment (one of which will be in a special school, the second in a mainstream school) who will be the experimental groups and a third group of pupils in mainstream school who do not have sensory impairments and who will act as a control. The two experimental groups will receive the teaching input while the control group will not. If the control group shows as much improvement as the experimental group in post-testing then it is highly unlikely that the teaching is responsible for the changes.

Again we will turn to ANOVA (see Example 4.2) in order to test whether or not any differences found were statistically significant and not just a fluke.

Further reading
Breakwell, G. *et al.* (1995) *Research Methods in Psychology*, London: Sage. (Chapter 7)

Qualitative approach

In the qualitative alternative we have suggested direct observation of a pupil using an event-focused study. Here the object is to track a pupil for a 'normal' school week and record the level of support she/he receives. This may seem straightforward, but there are a number of issues to consider. Systematic observation is certainly not an easy option.

Firstly, you might consider *how* you will observe the pupil. Will you observe from a distance (non-participant observer) or be involved in what is going on (participant observer)? Either way you will have to take account of how your presence might affect outcomes. If teachers are aware that you are looking to see when and how a pupil is supported then your presence is likely to affect their (and the pupils') normal activity (Hawthorn effect – see, Roethlisberger and Dickson 1939). If you opt to be involved in what is going on, that in itself may be perceived to be supportive and may therefore alter the way in which the pupil normally responds.

Second, if you were to record every single occurrence at every part of the day, apart from the logistical problems you will end up with a mountain of data. As a result it is more normal to *sample* situations or behaviours. There are many ways of sampling but the most common in this type of study are time and event sampling.

Time sampling involves recording what the pupil is doing at set time intervals (every 5 minutes for instance). Event sampling involves recording the details of an event from start to finish. In order to do this successfully you need to be clear about what constitutes an 'event' before embarking on the study. In our example you might wish to consider only events where teachers and/or other pupils offer 'task-focused' as opposed to 'general or social' support. In recording the support you must again decide whether you (or someone else) will record who supports, what they offer and for how long or alternatively record the language of support.

In order for support to be of value it has to be perceived as such by the recipient, so a second part of your task might be to ask pupils which interactions or resources they perceived as supportive and which they thought were not. You might also want to examine the degree to which pupils and teachers agreed or differed in their perceptions of what activities are supportive. In a study by Chaplain and Freeman (1994) this mismatching of perceived support among pupils with SEN and their teachers and carers was related to the stress experienced by those involved.

Further reading

Chaplain, R. and Freeman, A. (1994) *Caring Under Pressure*, London: David Fulton Publishers.

Foster, P. (1996) *Observing Schools: A methodological guide*, London: Paul Chapman Publishing.

Roethlisberger, F. J. and Dickson, W. J. (1939) *Management and the Worker*, Cambridge (MA): Harvard University Press.

Critical approach

The quality of interpersonal relationships between teachers and their pupils is seen as a central component of motivation and task engagement for both. While most teachers would argue that they treat all pupils equally, there is evidence to show that we unwittingly project differential messages to pupils and vice versa (Chaplain 1995b). Many of these messages are not concerned with what we say but rather the way in which we say it or the non-verbal actions that accompany what we say. There are a number of instruments available on the market to systematically observe teacher-pupil interaction, one of the most well known being *Flanders' Interaction Analysis* (Flanders 1970) to which we will refer in the following discussion.

Flanders' system provides the observer with ten categories of interaction, including teacher talk (divided into indirect (categories 1, 2, 3 and 4) and direct (categories 5, 6 and 7), student talk (categories 8 and 9) and silence (category 10). The observer simply records every three seconds what category best fits the classroom talk at that time. The results are recorded as strings of numbers (see Table

4.2). The system was generated from theories about group leadership and productivity. Although the collected data is quantitative it can be analysed either statistically or qualitatively. Thus the number and types of interaction can give some impression of the teaching style employed. In our research example we might contrast the profiles of teachers within schools and between schools (e.g. compare mainstream with special).

Table 4.2 An example of the type of form used to record data on teacher–pupil interaction using Flanders' (1970) categories

Interval (seconds)	Behaviour category									
30	5	5	5	5	5	5	5	5	5	5
60	5	5	5	5	9	9	9	9	2	2
90	2	2	5	5	5	8	8	8	3	3
120	4	4	4	5	5	5	6	6	6	6
150	7	7	8	5	5	7	7	9	9	9

While Flanders' instrument offers one perspective – the categorisation of talk and silence – it provides little information on the non-verbal behaviour taking place. To investigate this aspect you would utilise a different approach using photographic or video data for instance (see McLarty and Gibson 2000). You may decide to video the whole social episode and analyse both verbal and non-verbal behaviours at the same time.

Further reading
Boydell, D. and Jasman, A. (1983) *The Pupil and Teacher Record: A manual for observers*, Leicester University.
Chaplain, R. (1995b) 'Making a strategic withdrawal: disengagement and self-worth protection in male pupils' in J. Rudduck *et al.* (eds) *School Improvement: What can pupils tell us?* London: David Fulton Publishers.
Croll, P. 1986) *Systematic Classroom Observation*, London: Falmer.
Flanders, N. (1970) *Analysing Teacher Behaviour*, Reading, M.A: Addison Wesley.
McLarty, M. and Gibson, J.W. (2000) 'Using video technology in emancipatory research,' *European Journal of Special Needs Education* 13 (2), 138–148.

Developing a research theme

Research activity is a natural, dynamic and ongoing process. Some psychologists (e.g. Kelly 1955) argue that everybody acts like a naïve scientist trying to understand their worlds by making and testing hypotheses about the perceived causes of behaviour. Thus, it is hardly surprising that when working in schools this natural inquisitiveness is ever present. When embarking on a research project it is usual to end the report/paper with a statement on the limitations of the study and to suggest ways of 'filling in the gaps' among the results. This can often mean carrying out another project using a different methodology or sample in order to further confirm or rather provide more evidence to show why your findings should not be rejected.

In the above examples, and as illustrated in Table 4.1, we demonstrated the usefulness of examining research questions across two dimensions – at different levels and from different methodological viewpoints. Similarly, in deciding where to go next with your line of enquiry you may find that reference to Table 4.1 is of assistance. Taking the worked examples on inclusion, for instance, provides a two dimensional example of where you might start your study as well as different questions you might ask at different levels of analysis and activity. There is no simple logic to this since there is no telling where your results might lead nor what priorities and limitations will affect you, and Table 4.1 offers a comprehensive range of alternatives from which a larger scale study could be planned in a modular way.

Further reading
Kelly, G. A. (1955) *The Psychology of Personal Constructs, Volumes 1 and 2*, New York: Norton.

Additional references on research method

Bell, J. (1999) *Doing Your Research Project: A guide for first-time researchers in education and social science*, 3rd. edn, Buckingham: Open University Press.
Blaxter, L. *et al.* (1996) *How to Research*, Buckingham: Open University Press.
Brown, A. and Dowling, P. (1998) *Doing Research/Reading Research: A Mode of interrogation for education*, London: Falmer Press.
Cohen, L. and Manion, L. (2000) *Research Methods in Education*, 5th edn, London: Routledge.
Freeman, D. (1998) *Doing Teacher Research: From inquiry to understanding*, Pacific Grove: Heinle and Heinle Publishers.
Greene, J. and D'Oliveira, M. (1995) *Learning to Use Statistical Tests in Psychology*, Buckingham: Open University Press.
Hitchcock, G. and Hughes, D. (1995) *Research and the Teacher: A qualitative introduction to school-based research*, 2nd edn, London: Routledge.

CHAPTER 5

Research in practice

Figure 5.1 Outline of Chapter 5

In our final chapter we move on to look at presenting and applying the results of a school-based research project. After all, having spent a considerable time wrestling with concepts and doing fieldwork you are likely to want to see your findings being used to improve the quality of education for pupils with SEN. The chapter focuses on five main themes (Figure 5.1):

- Interpreting and writing up your findings;
- Disseminating research findings to others;
- Putting research into practice;
- Personal and professional development;
- Reflection and moving forward.

Interpreting and writing up your findings

There can be a significant pause between the collection, description and analysis of data, and its interpretation. One reason for this is that having been carried along with the processes of 'doing fieldwork', analysing interviews and observations, and producing summary notes, diagrams and tables of results, it is easy to lose sight of your intended outcomes. We might restate the processes involved in research as being concerned with the answers to the following questions:

- What's happening here?
- How do all the components fit together?
- What does it all mean?

These three questions are not hard-edged, and there can be considerable overlap between them. In Chapter 4 we discussed a number of ways to approach the first two questions and here we begin to examine the third – interpretation.

One question you might ask yourself, particularly when you are immersed in your results and wondering where you might go next is 'what's the story?' – in other words:

What are you trying to say?
What was your original question?
What information do you need to get across to the reader?
What is the purpose of your study?

Whatever type of research you engage in and whatever type of data that approach produces, its interpretation is inevitably a story of some sort. The task for the researcher is to transform the story into something more erudite or as Josselson and Lieblich (1993) put it: 'transform story material from the journalistic or literary to the academic and theoretically enriching' (p. xi).

In collecting and presenting data we often end up with much more material than we had originally expected, which increases our options and choices (and confusion). It's a little like being a child in a toy shop deciding what to ask for at Christmas – each successive row of glorious packaging offers something else which seems even more exciting than the last, so the list gets longer and longer. However, just as decisions will have to be made about which presents will (and will not) be bought for our imaginary child the same is the case for research data. Drawing the line is sometimes not easy. As a researcher you have set about trying to discover answers to a specific question (or questions), but finding something additional and interesting (but not necessarily part of your original question) can be seductive. Experienced researchers become less hooked on collecting data and more skilful at using the data they collect.

One way of keeping on track is to describe your findings to a *critical friend*. This does not mean merely showing them your expertly drawn tables and graphs, but rather explaining to them what you believe you have observed and discovered. Critical friends do not necessarily have to be technically aware of what it is you are researching. In fact, choosing individuals who are not in the teaching profession can often be a bonus, since such a choice is likely to require you to demonstrate your understanding of the data more clearly. After all the picture they manufacture in their minds will be limited to the account you have provided – as opposed to the interpretations they might make with first-hand experience.

This review process can be a powerful mechanism for interpreting your findings, since it can encourage you to focus on the key points, help you to dispense with unnecessary information, and stand back from the data in order to gain a wider view. Generally speaking it is healthy to ask critical friends to comment on your work as it develops, since this ongoing process can help you to keep things in perspective. At the same time, it is also important to maintain a balance between your own views and those of others. If you ask people to comment on your work, the feedback is likely to open yet more doors – some of which may not have occurred to you and which then require you to make further decisions about what (if anything) you should change and how to move forward. Again asking yourself 'what's the story' can be helpful in keeping your original questions in focus.

Remember also that *all* readers of your work will form their own interpretations, and that this process does not end when you write it up or even publish it. There is nothing more sobering than to read an essay or article written by someone else who makes reference to your findings and places an altogether different interpretation on what (you thought) you had originally said!

The research approach you select will inevitably influence the manner in which you interpret the data. In quantitative research you will have structured your plans for data analysis *before* commencing the study, and this will influence how and what data you collect. In contrast, some qualitative research approaches require you to build a model from fairly unstructured data – interpreting a tape-recorded discussion among a group of pupils, for instance. So the researcher must decide what is important from a mass of data (given that each component, it might be argued, has an importance of its own), and how to present it most effectively and interpret the findings. A second issue is how to determine the balance between description, analysis and interpretation. While analysis is closely bound to description, interpretation allows greater freedom. This does not mean however, that one can draw inferences where no link to the recorded data can be made – the link must be made clear. You should therefore resist the temptation to go too far beyond your description and analysis in drawing inferences or suggesting implications. In the end, the balance of description, analysis and interpretation (or speculation) depends upon the nature of the study and the intended uses for the findings.

Early in your writing up you should indicate the limitations of your study, including an indication of its contextual nature and to what extent the results can be generalised (see Bassey (1999) for a discussion of the 'fuzzy generalisation' which is involved in the application of research findings to different school contexts). Making this clear at the beginning of your study saves having to repeat it elsewhere. This is not intended as some form of insurance or disclaimer, but rather to make clear to the reader your understanding of the context in which the study was carried out and any special considerations that should be taken into account if, for instance, your study took place in a specialist residential facility with in-house specialist staff as opposed to a mainstream environment.

There are a number of ways in which data may be interpreted, ranging from the cautious to the more radical. At one extreme of the former the emphasis is on providing a number of possible explanations for your findings without committing to any particular one. At the other extreme one might attempt to demonstrate a relationship between a small-scale study and larger studies. In education research for instance, you might attempt to interpret your study within a 'bigger' theory in social science. The first step is to make sure you have visited and revisited your description and analysis and asked yourself (and your critical friends) what does it *mean* to you and them? Ask yourself:

- What patterns and links exist in the data?
- What differences are there between different elements of the sample?
- How do your findings compare with what others have found?

Getting started

The most important activity in writing up your study is (believe or not!) committing pen (or PC) to paper. It is only when you are actually in the process of constructing sentences or mind maps and the like that the project will begin to take something of a completed form. We are often plagued with distractions and rituals which detract us from this process. Making sure that you have your favourite writing implement to hand; that the paper is of the right texture; that you have checked your emails; you have a stock of highlighters and so on, serve as 'effective' displacement activities while you assemble your masterpiece. Needless to say, we all approach writing in very different ways and none is better nor worse than another – providing of course you have something to show for it at the end. As Becker

(1986) once said there is 'no one right way' of writing in social science research.

Some individuals are very methodical and can generate and hang on to the 'big picture' of what they plan to produce. Others work in shorter bursts of more frenzied activity when an idea strikes them. Many of these differences reflect our individual personalities and learning styles. Our advice is to get as much down on paper as you can and be prepared to edit and re-edit a number of times before expecting to complete your work. If you start out trying to write a perfectly presented piece of work from scratch, your chances of success are significantly less than if you accept that your ideas may not gel at the first, second or even third attempt. At least with something written down on paper you can begin to engage with it and revise your thinking. Be prepared to unpack, repack and discard (some of) your early sentences and thoughts a number of times along the way. It is often quite painful, if not uncommon among writers, to discard material which initially seemed very important. Yet this process is essential if you are to keep yourself, and ultimately the reader, focused on what it is you *need* to say, as opposed to reporting everything.

When writing it is not unusual to find yourself using far too many or far too few words to explain a particular piece of information. One ready check on this is to ask yourself 'how would I convey this information if I were *telling* someone else?' If there's no one around to do this with try using a tape recorder and listen to it yourself.

Spreading the word: disseminating your findings to others

Having described, analysed and interpreted your data the next question is how to write up your findings? There are two key questions here which relate to each other: What style should be adopted? Who is the target audience?

In answering the first question it is important to remember that while a number of recognised protocols exist when writing up a piece of research (see for example Cohen and Manion 2000), there is no *one* right way as we pointed out earlier. A glance through most educational research journals for instance, will reveal a range of different ways of presenting the results of both large and small projects. Those reporting heavily numerical analyses will often use a series of diagrams and/or tables to summarise large amounts of complex data. Qualitative studies will tend to have a more narrative style, but in many cases there is overlap between the two. Whatever type of research you are reporting, and whoever your intended audience, you will need to make explicit certain essential information, including:

- A rationale for the study – why did you decide to carry out the project in the first place?
- Literature review – what is known about this subject already?

- Operationalise your definitions – e.g. what criteria identify a 'reading difficulty'?
- Method – how did you collect your information?
- Results – what did you find and how did you analyse it?
- Discussion – what are your key findings and interpretations, and how do they relate to other people's findings? What are the limitations of your study?

The above list is familiar rather than novel but it still needs attention if you are to be able to put forward your case confidently, whether you are reporting the results to your colleagues or writing for an academic journal. For example, failure to look at existing literature on a subject may mean wasting considerable time wrestling with a problem which has already been addressed several times (producing your own measurement scale, for instance, when a usable one already exists). It will also indicate where contemporary research in the field is currently progressing in terms of focus and methodology.

Having spent valuable time completing your study it is usual to consider ways of getting the message across to those who might find your results useful in practical and/or conceptual ways. Listed below are a number of groups of people who might express different interests in your research. How the materials are presented and what is emphasised will differ between groups. Other practitioners in your field may value pragmatic or applied presentations, whereas more theoretical frameworks are likely to be demanded by academic journals. However, this is not intended to belittle practical research alongside a more glorious image of academia: theory and practice are not mutually exclusive. As the famous psychologist Kurt Lewin once said 'there is nothing so practical as a good theory!'

The following list covers some of the groups to whom you might wish to feedback your results:

Colleagues

Feedback often occurs through staff meetings (informal and formal) and as part of staff development and training days. Be adventurous in raising the status of research in the school by encouraging others to share their observations, and using this to help them develop their own investigations. You might go on to suggest that certain staff meetings are dedicated to considering how research might be used as part of personal and institutional development. To do this requires you to demonstrate the potential advantages of using research in this way. Here you might use other people's published research as well as your own to make the case.

Parents

Parents are generally interested in matters relating to their children's welfare and education and so involving them in the research process can provide valuable insight into your own findings, in addition to demonstrating your respect for their role in the educational process. At what point and in what types of research, you feedback to parents (or other adults outside of your own school) will depend on the nature of your existing relationships with them as well as your own feelings of competence and self-confidence in doing so – but don't be discouraged. Perhaps as part of a parents' evening you could organise a concurrent activity for interested parents to see what you have been doing – in the form of a poster display, video or short talk to present your results (most academic conference papers only last about 15 minutes). And don't just leave it there – encourage feedback, perhaps short written comments initially to find out if they would be interested in further involvement. Adding a carer's perspective to your work can be potentially stimulating to both the research process as well as to pupils' learning. Don't expect instant miracles and be prepared for some hard questioning on sensitive issues.

Pupils

Pupils are often asked to complete questionnaires or take part in interviews but on many occasions they receive very little feedback. Given that in many instances the pupils are the 'subjects' of research, they have significant investment in it and so should be treated accordingly (i.e. as 'participants' rather than subjects). When carrying out school-based surveys, we never cease to be amazed how many pupils write thanking for having provided them with, first, the chance to make a comment and second, feedback on what we found. When planning a project make an effort to build in time for feedback to participants and treat it seriously. You might wish to incorporate pupil (and other) feedback into your research report.

Governors

As managers of a school governors are usually keen to hear about what is going on so keep them informed. Governors are often in a position to support fund-raising which might be used to support research activity.

Local Education Authorities

While the relationship between schools and LEAs has changed in recent years, they still represent key players in the schooling process, certainly in terms of holding considerable data and expertise in the form of advisers and other officers. Sharing your findings can pay dividends in terms of getting hold of further information to develop your research theme at a different level. LEAs can also have an important role in setting up teacher research networks for colleagues in different schools (Flutter *et al.* 1998).

Higher education institutions

Many schools have strong links with HE institutions and thus should have developed or be in the process of developing ways of shared dissemination of research findings from both sides. If you don't have a working relationship with your nearest HE establishment make the first move. Get hold of a staff list, contact relevant lecturers and encourage their involvement. Ask if they have a research network or run research seminars, and get involved where you can. A partnership between schools and higher education is built into the various research projects initiated by the Teacher Training Agency (www.canteach.gov.uk).

Publishing

There are a number of ways in which you can publish your work to a wider audience. There are hundreds of different journals in the market each of which has its own *raison d'être*. Most journals include details of how to meet publishing requirements (usually inside the cover) which indicate their preferred topics, target audiences, length, style and how to present your article (see Table 5.1 for some examples). If you plan to publish your research (and there is no reason why you should not) you will need to familiarise yourself with the range of journals available and which one your research report might fit. Journals include practice orientated weekly/monthly publications on for example, special needs, teaching approaches and curriculum issues. Articles in such journals tend to be relatively short (two or three pages) aimed at teachers and containing practical help and guidance. At the other extreme are relatively long articles (7000+ words) in refereed academic journals, which are usually published two or three times per year. In between the two are a vast range of other publications with different emphases on the level of theoretical and applied content.

Books

As with journals, emphases in books differ. Some have an applied focus while others are more academic. If your research is practical in nature (e.g. curriculum materials, teaching approaches) you might consider producing materials for schools which are published as pamphlets or in books which can be photocopied. There are a number of publishers who specialise in this type of publication – materials in your own school will provide some ideas. Publishers will usually expect you to produce sample materials for review including a contents list, sample chapters or worksheets, and some indication of length.

Table 5.1 A range of journals publishing educational research findings

Journal title	Number of issues per year	Maximum article length (no. of words)
British Journal of Special Education	4	not stated
British Educational Research Journal	5	not stated
Cambridge Journal of Education	3	6000
Education 3–13	3	2–4000
Education Today	4	1000 or c.3000
European Journal of Special Needs Education	3	4–7000
International Journal of Inclusive Education	4	not stated
Research in Education	2	2–500 or c.3500
Special Children	9	not stated (2–3 pages)
Special! (NASEN)	3	not stated (2–3 pages)
Support for Learning	4	not stated

Making your research count: putting research into practice

Assuming you have found something which you believe should be disseminated to colleagues and put into practice, then there are a number of considerations to keep in mind. These considerations can be viewed under four related headings (see also Chapter 2 for a discussion of issues relating to research and professional practice):

- Personal – including your motives for engaging in the research; previous research and teaching experience; professional role and status in school.
- Interpersonal/intergroup – including the perceptions of your project (and research in general) and the level of support among your colleagues; the formal and informal communication systems and procedures for collaboration and sharing of ideas.
- Organisational – including the current school development plan; degree of support from the senior management team (SMT); status and cultural role of research in your school.
- External factors – including working relationships between your school and others (locally and nationally); external pressures on school and national initiatives; relationships within the LEA; membership of teacher research networks and partnerships with research institutions such as universities.

Practical issues

- Remember that the process of applying your results has an inherent evaluative component which can often lead to further research (involving, for instance, overcoming obstructions to implementing new initiatives; extending your sample; changing methods of evaluation; forming new hypotheses).
- Try and keep some control over the process of applying your findings. Having been meticulous with your analysis and interpretation, don't allow others to make spurious claims or extend beyond what you can confidently defend.
- Translate your conclusions into workable targets preferably with shorter and longer term outcomes. Short-term, manageable targets are best taken on board first, since if people can achieve early success they are more likely to persevere with longer term goals.
- Ensure that feedback systems are in place and explicit so that people can see the results, problems and secondary targets clearly.
- Plan and monitor evaluation systems and make their findings accessible to those involved – keep the project alive!
- Remember, change can be both stimulating and/or stressful, and it occurs in stages. Talking about change, making it happen and sustaining it, generate very different problems.
- If you are not a member of the SMT make sure you have at least one member involved in the process of applying your results.
- If a working party is being used to develop your ideas make sure that the outcomes are kept clear and up front. Try to avoid getting hung-up with means at the expense of ends!

Personal and professional development

Doing research in school can be seen as part of a lifelong process of learning about children, teaching and education in general. Usually, research emerges from 'what I already know'; it is planned around 'what I want to find out'; and it inevitably leads to questions about how to address 'what I still don't know'.

It is not only the interests (and confusions) which remain after completing a research project which trigger attempts to gather more information and develop further knowledge and understanding. The early stages of collecting one's thoughts about 'what I already know' are also likely to involve searches for relevant information and alternative views about the research topic. Indeed, the time spent on discussing the research questions and reading as much as possible is central to working out the main ideas which will guide the study. This is commonly a trail-like process of following references and developing an understanding of how different topics and questions connect, and it can take more time than you might think (see *Speaking from experience . . .* below). The advantages of investing time for this usually become very clear as the project proceeds, especially in terms of the growing feeling of being on top of the field and having something to tell others. It can build a lot of confidence to have the experience of picking up another book and suddenly realising that you recognise the names; you understand the concepts; you are automatically evaluating other people's research in the light of what you know; you have research evidence to contribute; and you have a well-informed opinion about the issues arising. However, it is also important to decide when to *stop* following the trail, and begin the research or the writing up.

Speaking from experience . . . Learning about early reading and writing:
Here are some extracts from notes written by Bea Doubleday, a reception class teacher, embarking on a research dissertation to complete an Advanced Diploma in Early Years Education. Her literature search and reading stretched over a period of two to three months. (All references have been omitted.)

> I was initially interested in finding out about whether there was a link between a child's drawing of a person and their readiness to read. I remembered during my teacher training in the seventies, that we were taught that it was possible to tell when a child was ready to read ('reading readiness'), and that one of the ways to tell this was by looking at their drawing of a person . . . I began by reading books about the early drawings of children and trying to see whether there was still thought to be this link. There were references which linked children's pictures to early language and to the ability to share and communicate thoughts, feelings and ideas . . . but it was difficult to find relevant information which linked drawing to reading, and it was beginning to be apparent to me that the missing link was the early writing . . . I decided to make a collection of drawings of people which each child did during their first week of school, and use these to study the ways that they were able to represent a person . . . I also decided to see what I could find out about 'reading readiness'. At this stage I was thinking about whether I could devise a test that I could use with my named children . . . I naturally found many references to the link between reading and writing, but not to the possible links between reading and drawing . . . After consultation with my tutor I decided to look further into the connection with writing and see if I could research the link between drawing, writing and reading . . . Two things were soon repeating themselves over and over again in my reading. Firstly, the use of the word 'symbolic' in relation to all forms of activities of the young child, not just literacy. Secondly, the fact that literacy is part of the whole child and their experiences . . . At this point I began to think about literacy as a whole-person approach and felt that I had become too narrow . . . In one of the journals I found an article which argued that all early childhood educators must

understand how important imaginative play is for the child's cognitive development. The author felt that this is crucial to the understanding of symbolic representation which in turn is necessary for the development of early literacy . . . I began to be increasingly interested in the part that role-play has in the young child's understanding of symbolism and how this leads into the sound/symbol correspondence needed for writing and reading. Language, both speech and writing, is a system of symbols, where one thing stands for another . . .

(This led to Bea's final decisions about how to focus her research in school, looking at the links between young children's early writing and symbolic representation in play and drawing.)

Information-finding and learning

There are several different ways of finding relevant information, however, as we know, possessing information does not necessarily lead to greater knowledge and understanding. The information has to be read, interpreted, evaluated and used to build the network of ideas which already exist – i.e. it is a process of *learning*. The way that this happens varies. There is a strong social aspect to learning in that we are flooded with persuasive arguments in the media, we discuss ideas with other people, and we use language and cultural concepts and beliefs to help us describe and understand the world (although the continuing debates about the meaning of SEN show that we do not all share the same views). In that sense it is not possible to develop knowledge and understanding in isolation. However, our actual experiences of learning are not the same. Research into individual differences in 'learning styles' and 'learning preferences' (Riding and Rayner 1998) suggests a number of dimensions or alternative tendencies. As with the processes of writing up discussed earlier, some people may tend to form a view of the whole picture while others build up understanding step-by-step; some people gain a lot from diagrams, while others prefer to read straightforward text; some learn best collaboratively and others more independently; some prefer a warm, quiet room and others the opposite, etc. The point is that the sources of information outlined below have to be seen as different starting points for *learning*. This means that while one person would do best in going to the library for a week and reading anything that looks interesting, another person may prefer to discuss the topic informally with several different people and then search for specific articles using a research database. One of the authors of this book finds that reading around the subject is often best followed by a shopping trip to allow the ideas to percolate without thinking too much about it! The information-finding skills which we all gain over the years work best in the context of knowing how we each learn and building in opportunities to learn in our own ways.

Sources of information

- *other people*

The quickest way to find information can be to ask someone – a colleague, parents, children, etc. There is a wide network of information and advice available for teachers. Parents and children will usually know a great deal about a syndrome or medical condition, for example, often supported by their own contacts with relevant voluntary groups. School colleagues will have knowledge to share from their own teaching or from attendance at courses. This may be formalised in staff development sessions, or discussed more informally from day-to-day. Local inspectors and advisers can be helpful in their own area, as can colleagues in other schools and educational institutions. A valuable means of rapid communication with teacher colleagues is through membership of a well-supported email discussion group such as senco-forum (see the BECTA (British Educational Communications and Technology Agency) website (Inclusion and SEN page): www.becta.org.uk). Messages to senco-forum frequently ask for specific information and receive several replies by the next day. Courses and conferences can also be useful sources of information and contact, as they intend. Educational conferences such as those run by the British Educational Research Association (www.bera.ac.uk) and the National Association for Special Educational Needs (www.nasen.org.uk), are now finding ways of involving more practising teachers – often simply by making provision for one-day attendance with a clearly relevant focus to the programme, and publicising to a wider audience in schools. Short courses and college- or school-based longer diplomas and higher degrees can be life-changing, not just from the information delivered but through the active experience of choosing to learn together with other course members (and often in this way gaining knowledge well beyond the course curriculum).

- *educational support services, professional associations and voluntary groups*

Material floods into schools from national and local organisations – including catalogues, reports, curriculum guidance, policy documents, etc. For example, the Index for Inclusion (a staff development file published by the Centre for Studies on Inclusive Education (CSIE 2000)) was sent to schools by the DfEE. However, knowing that there is likely to be something relevant somewhere in school is not the same as knowing which shelf it is actually sitting on, so it is worth being clear about the distribution system in school. Teachers' Centres may be less common now, but local education authority support and advisory services have their own reference materials available to teachers (e.g. about Traveller Education, ICT, specific learning difficulties, etc.). Education exhibitions give access to a range of organisations and publishers, and they can be a quick way to get hold of a range of catalogues and try out materials and software – well attended examples include BETT (the British Educational Technology Show), the annual Education Show in Birmingham, and NASEN exhibitions. Memberships of professional associations and unions have the advantage of providing access to up-to-date information about general educational issues. Charities and voluntary groups offer specific information and advice, several with campaigning approaches which tackle key issues such as inclusion and which offer rapid explanations of and responses to legal and political initiatives (e.g. IPSEA, the Independent Panel for Special Education Advice, www.ipsea.org.uk). The addresses for a wide variety of specific organisations such as the Association of Workers for Children with Emotional and Behavioural Difficulties (AWCEBD), the British Dyslexia Association (BDA), and the British Association for Teachers of the Deaf (BATOD) can be found via the BECTA website, Inclusion and SEN page (www.becta.org.uk).

● *newspapers, professional journals, TV and radio*

Regular reading of newspapers can pay off in the summaries of relevant research findings and new initiatives. These may be on a dedicated page (as in the 'Research Focus' of the *Times Educational Supplement* (*TES*), or included as features in the *TES* and other broadsheets. Certain professional journals include news pages and course/conference listings as well as articles about research and practice (e.g. *Special Children* produced by Questions Publishing; *Special!* from NASEN). There are also relevant newsletters available by subscription, such as the *Special Needs Information Press* (www.snip-newsletter.co.uk). TV and radio often come up with useful documentaries, usually on topical subjects such as ADHD, and there are of course the Open University broadcasts.

● *books, academic journals and the internet*

Books about SEN and inclusion continue to appear and it is worth browsing regularly in an academic bookshop. Garner and Robinson (2000) recently identified 47 books about SEN which primary teachers had found memorable and useful. However much educational research is published in journals and reports. In their guidance for educational research writing, the British Educational Research Association (BERA 2000) draws up a pyramid model of connected writings, ranging from a full report of the research giving sufficient detail for replication and audit, to academic papers accredited through peer review, to professional reports written for policy makers or practitioners, to brief news reports intended to attract attention to the study. Sometimes this range of possibilities for publication becomes apparent in looking at one study. For example, a chapter about a recent research project on Teacher Support Teams (Daniels *et al.* 2000) refers to several different reports of the same project written for the funding body and as papers in academic journals. The study was also publicised in professional journals and the *TES*, as well as in a book for teachers (Creese *et al.* 1997).

Academic journals tend to be less immediately accessible than books, although well-used British publications such as the *British Journal of Special Education* and *Support for Learning* are available with membership of NASEN. For academic journals, the main access is through university and college libraries and occasionally on the internet. A new venture, the online *Journal of Research in SEN*, is starting up in 2001 with three issues a year (available by subscription from NASEN: www.nasen.org.uk).

Browsing is often very effective (the last two years' issues of an academic journal from the shelf can be scanned for articles of interest in about 15 minutes), however systematic searches are frequently necessary if you are not lucky enough to find a recent review of research on your topic in a journal (or try the BERA Map of Educational Research, www.bera.ac.uk). Library catalogues can be searched for book titles, key phrases, subject areas and authors (but not for chapter titles in an edited book). They can also be searched for the titles of journals held in the library. Access to journal articles is gained through databases such as the British Education Index (BEI) or ERIC (the Educational Resources Information Center, based in the USA). The BEI has a quarterly hard copy version which can be searched by author and subject, and it is also available on CD-ROM and as a searchable online database which can extract the abstracts of selected articles. See Smeaton (1999) for detailed information about library searches in the field of education.

Searching books, journals and the internet needs a creative approach, with some precision, persistence and lateral thinking. It is also important to be aware of what each source of information can and cannot offer. To give an example, here are the first three hits from a search (in January 2001) for 'dyslexia' using an internet search engine, the BEI (online), the University of Cambridge School of Education library catalogue, and the *TES* archives. As you see, the results include relevant organisations, academic articles, videos, books, newspaper reports and book reviews:

Search engine: Google (www.google.com)
1. Dyslexia: The Gift. Information and Resources for Dyslexia (www.dyslexia.com)
2. British Dyslexia Association (www.bda-dyslexia.org.uk)
3. The Dyslexia Institute (www.dyslexia-inst.org.uk)

British Education Index (online)
1. Lehtola, R. and Lehto, J. E. (2000) 'Assessing dyslexia in Finnish high-school students: a pilot study', *European Journal of Special Needs Education* 15 (3), 255–263.
2. Orr, S. (2000) 'Lecturers' conceptions of students with literacy difficulties', *College Research* 3 (3), 40–42.

3. Landerl, K. and Wimmer, H. (2000) 'Deficits in phoneme segmentation are not the problem of dyslexia: evidence from German and English children', *Applied Psycholinguistics* 21 (2), 243–262.

University of Cambridge School of Education Library (www.cam.ac.uk)

1. A video: *Dyslexia in the Primary Classroom* (BBC 1997)
2. A video: *Dyslexic Children* (Channel 4 1999)
3. Keates, A. (2000) *Dyslexia and Information and Communications Technology: A guide for teachers and parents,* London: David Fulton Publishers.

Times Educational Supplement archives (www.tes.org.uk) (a whole archive search, but it is possible to select certain sections)
1. A news report on the launch of a BDA campaign 'It Matters', for adult dyslexics
2. A news report on a national themed competition called 'As I See IT', inviting contributions of prose, poetry, painting, photography, film, website design, etc., by the BDA and the Dyslexia Institute
3. A review by Martin Turner, head of psychology at the Dyslexia Institute, of four recently published resource packs and books for teachers.

Reflection and moving forward

Reflection as part of the research process: speaking from experience . . .

It is not only action research which involves reflection as part of the research process. Other forms of research also require the researcher to stand back from the situation, to interpret and evaluate what is happening, and to decide how to move forward. This can involve looking into one's own feelings and motivations for continuing, especially in the face of dilemmas and obstacles (Kershner 1999). In this book we have offered what we hope is useful information and advice about doing school-based research, but individual circumstances and experiences vary. So we invited some teachers to write down their own reflections on school-based research, including some advice for other teacher researchers. They are speaking from their own experience . . .

Experiences of teacher researchers

Neil Toplass has a total of six years teaching experience, including five years in a mainstream infant school. He is now a Year 3 class teacher in a primary school for pupils with emotional and behavioural difficulties. The pupils are working at the equivalent of a level 1–2 early years curriculum, and Neil is beginning a research project with them on early reading and the use of ICT:

- ## *Why did you begin the research in the context of your responsibilities and interests as a teacher?*

I have always had an interest in how learning takes place . . . from animals to people to computers. After completing a psychology degree in 1991 this raised more questions than answers. However on entering the real world of employment, my interest took a back seat until 1998 when I was asked at my previous school to mentor student teachers . . . As a result I had the opportunity to reflect on all aspects of my teaching which inadvertently rekindled the flames of interest in ' how learning takes place'. When given the opportunity to support a research project initiated by Homerton College I jumped at the chance. On the back of this experience I considered what research or information would benefit my current working practices and placement with EBD children, who have a wide variety of complex learning difficulties and needs.

The school environment where I am now working provides greater opportunity to gain insight into learning strategies for a number of reasons:

1. The children are in small groups and have high staffing ratios, making it easier to conduct individual tests and assessments.
2. There is greater flexibility in the timetable (compared with mainstream), which allows children the time to experience and consolidate newly presented information.
3. There is greater opportunity to modify teaching practice than in mainstream to serve, more 'accurately', children's individual needs.

- ## *What are the benefits and problems?*

The benefits will hopefully be reaped when the research has been completed. It should provide accurate information about the individual children and their learning styles and how these are best met in all aspects of the classroom. In addition, it is beneficial in that it is making me look more closely and think more carefully about what is going on in the classroom and how I and other adults are part of this. It is also focusing my thoughts more clearly around what is being learnt by the children.

The disadvantages are largely time-related if things don't go as smoothly as planned. Having said that, so far there has been ample flexibility offered in meeting schedules etc. which has offset any major problems

- *How do you intend to use and disseminate the findings?*

Depending on the outcomes I would expect to produce (with help) a brief paper and provide opportunities to discuss findings and issues raised with fellow staff members and anyone else who is willing to listen.

- *Have you any tips for dealing with the dilemmas and practicalities?*

To plan in flexibility . . . particularly during the times when work is to be completed in school.

- *Is school-based research going to be an important part of teaching in the future?*

It has to be . . . in both mainstream and special schools. As technology evolves and political ideology changes, schools will be (and are) asked to provide an increasingly prescibed curriculum. The difficulty is that it may not be (and in an EBD school largely isn't) the way forward if learning is to be improved and accessible to all children . . . e.g. boys vs girls. The introduction of technology is also a massive issue, and not only for teachers who will need training to use it. Computers will be capable of even more amazing things in just five years from now. To understand what children actually learn from their interactions, needs to be evaluated in the classroom, alongside the teaching input over a period of time. This should then be reflected in how software and hardware is developed.

Linda Upham carried out research to complete an advanced diploma at Homerton College. She was then a Specialist Support Teacher, and is now Team Manager, Primary Support Service. Her dissertation was called 'The relevance of type face in the acquisition of reading skills', completed in 1998.

- *Why did you begin the research in the context of your responsibilities and interests as a teacher?*

My research was driven by the need to acquire a further recognised qualification in SEN which was itself the result of pressure by county council authorities to conform to government (TTA) guidelines relevant to the role of specialist support teacher. It also provided the opportunity to undertake a literature search into my chosen field; to update my knowledge and test a feeling about why some children were failing to acquire early reading skills.

- *What are the benefits and problems?*

The most important benefit to me personally and professionally was the opportunity to read a wide variety of publications and to discuss my ideas and thoughts with an interested and knowledgeable tutor who encouraged me to question ideas and beliefs and test them out. I rarely have any opportunity to reflect on practice set against the wider educational field and consider the far horizons of education, so I consider that the opportunity to study was a rare luxury.

The problems centred on permutations around time and availability of children to take part in the study:

1. Release time to do the literature survey and the practical testing necessary for the research was always a premium because of the cost of providing a supply teacher to cover my time out.
2. This was further compounded by the need for a supply teacher with specialist SEN expertise.
3. Most of the work sorting, organising and writing about the data had to be done in my own time and relied on the indulgence of my family.
4. Research on the children could only be done in school time.
5. I had to rely on the willingness of the schools and class teachers to allow children to miss elements of the curriculum when I was with them.
6. Although no parent refused permission for their child to take part, I was not prepared at first to have to speak to a parent and justify what I was doing.
7. Sanitising the data – removing names etc. – took far longer than I thought and I had to be careful that I didn't muddle the numbered groups when referring to them in the text.

- **How did you use and disseminate the findings, or how do you intend to do so?**

I used the dissertation to meet the requirements of my employment! However, it also raised my awareness of fonts and I have usually typed worksheets and other material in Sassoon if available, or in Arial, or as clear a font as possible. I have not disseminated my findings – lack of time to fully explore senco-forum or similar networks.

- **Have you any tips for dealing with the dilemmas and practicalities?**

1. Ensure that you have your family's support because it is going to eat into your spare time.
2. Allow twice as much time as you originally estimated to do the research to take account of sickness, school assemblies, red nose day and theatre visits. Double this if it looks like you are going to need to do further research (as I did).
3. Establish a good rapport and understanding with the head teacher and class teachers and fully explain what is involved in terms of access and time (where are you going to do this, how often) as well as what it is all about.

4. Be prepared to abandon your original hypothesis and follow interesting 'rabbit holes'.

5. Enjoy it!

- **Is school-based research going to be an important part of teaching in the future?**

It ought to be if we are to move practice forward, however, the usual constraints of lack of INSET time and money for longer periods of study will curtail this – part-time study over a year is not cheap. In addition the increasing need to show that research leads to a recognised qualification or piece of paper means that many people may not do small scale projects which could be of great practical use. There is a frustration level too – having found out what I needed to do next to extend my study and explore the idea further, I had to 'abandon' it and return to full-time work.

Sue Walsh currently works as a Learning Support Teacher and Assistant Head of Year at Clevedon Community School, North Somerset. As such she has had very close and recent experience of social inclusion as well as the increased inclusion of children with a wider range of learning needs. She has recently completed her MA Education (SEN) with the University of the West of England, Bristol. Her research study 'Inclusion – rhetoric or reality?' is an analysis of the factors which influence teachers' attitudes to the greater inclusion of children with learning differences and emotional difficulties in her mainstream secondary school.

- **Why did you begin the research in the context of your responsibilities and interests as a teacher?**

As a learning support teacher I was at the beginning of the school's first truly inclusive placement. i.e. that of a young man with severe learning difficulties (SLD). This was, as you can imagine, an enormous challenge for an SEN team and general staff who had had no training and were to receive little support. As his first year unfolded I was fascinated to see how different members of staff reacted towards him and was keen to examine the factors that ultimately influenced their attitudes to inclusion. One interpretation of inclusive responses involves whole school improvement, indicating that schools could and should change. Government agenda and existing support frameworks didn't really figure, my findings revealed that deep rooted and ostensibly unmoveable, socio-historic factors were the principal and most powerful influence on staff attitudes.

My role as Assistant Head of Year also meant that I was heavily involved in the pastoral team's responses to social inclusion. The greater inclusion of children with EBD impacted on the very essence of teachers' perception of professional self and above all self-esteem.

• What are the benefits and problems?

Benefits – enormous. Discussion with teachers from other schools at research seminars served to sharpen my understanding of issues and realise how unique each educational setting is. One size does not and cannot fit all! Trawling professional journals, educational press etc. further added to this. My understanding of how teachers tick and react to a range of factors has increased. Professionally, my perceptions of inclusion have become more realistic. Also more critical of present structures, strategies in school. It has been fascinating to see how some of the thoughts I have expressed in a number of forums have been taken up. Don't know whether this is coincidental or not!

Problems – diverse. Being a research practitioner often put me in an unrealistic position in my professional setting. Conducting and recording semi-structured interviews and sending out self-completion surveys was false. My role as a learning support teacher means that I am often in other people's classroom, at times I had to be careful that I was fulfilling that role and not that of a participant observer. This was not very easy. Taking field notes often felt like snooping even though I had requested staff cooperation when presenting my research proposal at a full staff meeting. Power relations figured due to gender, age, status in school figured. Particularly the pastoral/curriculum divide. Even more so the sub/para role that SEN has in school.

• How did you use and disseminate the findings? (or how do you intend to do so?)

A copy of my dissertation will be available for public scrutiny at the University of West of England's library. Ideally I would have liked to give a non-compulsary presentation of my research findings to the SMT/staff/governors of my school. I've requested this but have yet to have my offer taken up! I believe this may be because the school's priorities are not SEN related, perhaps if I had investigated a curriculum issue such as how to raise GCSE pass rates this would have been more palatable/marketable/less emotive.

Senco-forum has enabled me to post an abstract of my research study and there has been considerable interest in my findings from undergraduates, graduate students, those undertaking PhDs and post-doctoral research.

• Have you any tips for dealing with the dilemmas and practicalities?

Keep things in perspective. Follow recommended ethical guidelines about asking permission of colleagues and respecting their right to refuse to contribute. Find gentle ways of letting them off and don't hold it against them!! Don't smash and grab data and remember that even though you will have a growing passion for the study, many will just not be interested in what you are doing. Things do return to normal, it's often frustrating to have developed greater insights into what is happening in school and not be able to shout them out. Your contributions to all sorts of forums will be influenced by your findings, believe in yourself. It is quite fun to have the confidence to say 'but recent research reveals . . .'. A decision in my school to adopt a certain model of learning support may have been influenced by my ability to categorically say it didn't happen anywhere else!!

- ***Is school-based research going to be an important part of teaching in the future?***

The government wants it to be! Yes, most certainly. The present government's education agenda at its worse is severe and uninformed interventionitis. Too many reforms with little pragmatic insight and too little empirical evidence to support them. The whole inclusion movement is an excellent example, based on emotive human rights philosophy, it didn't really take account of the realities of the chalk face and the impact full inclusion would have on all the stakeholders, not least the children! As a profession if we want to have some ownership over the future of education, it's important that we feel that grass roots research is taken into account.

Considering further research

The end of a school-based project need not be the end of a teacher's involvement in research, although other practical responsibilities may have to take priority for a while. We have already discussed how research inevitably leaves specific questions and further interests in the area. The experience of school-based research can also lead to an interest in research itself. It can change the perception of teaching, so that research becomes a fundamental part of the job and the skills are added to the repertoire which allows teachers to teach well.

We discussed in Chapters 1 and 2 why teachers may begin school-based research for both personal and professional reasons. The end of a project can allow these reasons to become more focused and goal-directed. There may, for example, be specific school interests or needs expressed in the school development plan which can be addressed by school-based research. Individual teachers may wish to extend a small-scale project and work at different levels (pupils, adults, whole-school) or in different settings – perhaps as part of a teacher research network. This could involve bidding for financial support within school or through national programmes such as the Teacher Research Grant Scheme or Best Practice Research Scholarships (www.canteach.gov.uk or www.dfee.gov.uk/bprs). Teachers may also want to extend their own qualifications and gain an advanced diploma or higher degree. A masters degree may prepare the ground for the depth of study allowed by a PhD, or teachers may be attracted by one of the newer EdD (Doctor of Education) courses designed for professional workers in education. Teachers may also wish to support other colleagues in their own research, or act as mentors to trainees who may be tackling small-scale projects in school for a course assignment or dissertation, or contribute as tutors on courses for trainees and experienced teachers.

Educational research needs teachers to be actively involved, and teachers need opportunities and support to do so. The field of SEN and inclusion, with all its dilemmas, complexities and gaps in knowledge, can only benefit from the knowledge and understanding gained through the involvement of teachers in research and the dissemination of teachers' school-based research findings.

References

Adey, P. and Shayer, M. (1994) *Really Raising Standards: Cognitive intervention and academic achievement*, London: Routledge.

Ainscow, M. (1998) 'Would it work in theory? Arguments for practitioner research and theorising in the special needs field', in Clark, C. *et al.* (eds) *Theorising Special Education*, 7–20. London: Routledge.

Ainscow, M. (1999) *Understanding the Development of Inclusive Schools*, London: Falmer Press.

Al-Hilawani, Y. A. (2000) 'A new approach to evaluating metacognition in hearing average-achieving; "hearing underachieving"; and "deaf/hard of hearing" elementary school students', *British Journal of Special Education* 27 (1), 41–47.

Allebone, B. (1998) 'Providing for able children in the primary classroom', *Education 3–13* March Issue, 64–69.

Alton-Lee, A. *et al.* (2000) 'Inclusive practice within the lived cultures of school communities: research case studies in teaching, learning and inclusion', *Interational Journal of Inclusive Education* 4 (3), 179–210.

Armstrong, D. *et al.* (1998) 'From theory to practice: special education and the social relations of academic production', in Clark, C. *et al.* (eds) *Theorising Special Education*, 32–43. London: Routledge.

Ashman, A. F. and Conway, R. N. F. (1997) *An Introduction to Cognitive Education: Theory and applications*, London: Routledge.

Babbage, R. *et al.* (1999) *Approaches to Teaching and Learning: Including pupils with learning difficulties*, London: David Fulton Publishers.

Bannifer, D. and Fransella, F. (1974) *Inquiring Man: The psychology of personal constructs*, 3rd edn, London: Croom Helm.

Barber, M. (1994) 'Young people and their attitudes to school', An interim report of a research project in the Centre for Successful Schools (Keele University).

Barkley, R. A. (1990) *Attention Deficit Disorder: A handbook for diagnosis and treatment*, New York: The Guilford Press.

Barkley, R. A. (1997) *ADHD and the Nature of Self-Control,* New York: The Guilford Press.

Barnes, C. and Mercer, G. (eds.) (1997) *Doing Disability Research,* Leeds: The Disability Press.

Bassey, M. (1999) *Case Study Research in Educational Settings,* Buckingham: Open University Press.

Bayliss, P. (1998) 'Models of complexity: theory-driven intervention practices', in Clark, C. *et al.* (eds) *Theorising Special Education,* 61–78. London: Routledge.

Becker, H. S. (1986) *Writing for Social Scientists: How to start and finish your thesis, book or article,* Chicago: University of Chicago Press.

BERA (British Educational Research Association) (2000) *Good Practice in Educational Research Writing,* Southwell, Notts.: BERA.

Blamires, M. (ed.) (1999) *Enabling Technology for Inclusion,* London: Paul Chapman Publishing.

Blatchford, P. (1996) 'Pupils' views on school work and school from 7 to 16 years', *Research Papers in Education* **11** (3), 263–288.

Bozic, N. and Murdoch, H. (eds) (1996) *Learning Through Interaction: Technology and children with multiple disabilities,* London: David Fulton Publishers.

Braswell, L. and Bloomquist, M. L.(1991) *Cognitive-Behavioural Therapy with ADHD Children: Child, family and school intervention,* New York: Guildford Press.

Bronfenbrenner, U. (1992) 'Ecological systems theory', in Vasta, R. (ed.) *Six Theories of Child Development: Revised formulations and current issues,* 187–249. London: Jessica Kingsley Publishers.

Buckle, L. (1999) 'Every need is special', *Special Children* **117**, February, 9–12.

Chaney, L. E. and Bugental, D. B. (1982) 'An attributional approach to hyperactive behaviour', in Antaki, C. and Brewin, C. (eds*) Attributions and Psychological Change: Applications of attribution theories to clinical and educational practice,* 211–234. London: Academic Press.

Chaplain, R. (1995a) 'Stress and job satisfaction: a study of English primary teachers', *Educational Psychology* **15** (4), 473–489.

Chaplain, R. (1995b) 'Making a strategic withdrawal: disengagement and self-worth protection in male pupils' in J. Ruddick *et al.* (eds) *School Improvement: What can pupils tell us?* London: David Fulton Publishers.

Chaplain, R. (2000a) 'Helping children to persevere and be well motivated' in Whitebread,' (ed.) *The Psychology of Teaching and Learning in the Primary School,* 96–115. London: RoutledgeFalmer.

Chaplain, R. (2000b) 'Educating children with behaviour difficulties', Whitebread, D. (ed.) *The Psychology of Teaching and Learning in the Primary School,* 300–322. London: RoutledgeFalmer.

Chaplain, R. (2000c) 'Beyond exam results? Differences in the social and psychological perceptions of young males and females at school', *Educational Studies* 26 (2) 177–191.

Chaplain, R. and Freeman, A. (1994) *Caring Under Pressure*, London: David Fulton Publishing.

Children Act (1989) London: HMSO.

Clark, C. *et al.* (eds) (1998) *Theorising Special Education*, London: Routledge.

Clough, P. and Barton, L. (eds) (1995a) *Making Difficulties: Research and the construction of SEN*, London: Paul Chapman Publishing.

Clough, P. and Barton, L. (1995b) 'Introduction: self and the research act', in Clough P. and Barton L. (eds) *Making Difficulties: Research and the construction of SEN*, London: Paul Chapman Publishing.

Clough, P. and Barton, L. (eds) (1998) *Articulating with Difficulty: Research voices in inclusive education*, London: Paul Chapman Publishing.

Cohen, L. and Manion, L. (2000) *Research Methods in Education*, 5th edn. London: Routledge.

Collins, J. (1996) *The Quiet Child.* London: Cassell.

Cook, T. (1998) 'The importance of mess in action research', *Educational Action Research* 6, 93–108.

Cooper, P. and Bilton, K. (1999) *ADHD: Research, practice and opinion*, London: Whurr Publishers.

Cooper, P and Ideus, K. (2000) *Attention Deficit/Hyperactivity Disorder: A practical guide for teachers*, London: David Fulton Publishers.

Cooper, P. and Lovey, J. (1999) 'Early intervention in emotional and behavioural difficulties: the role of Nurture Groups', *European Journal of Special Needs Education* 14 (2), 122–131.

Corbett, J. (1996) *Bad-mouthing: The language of special needs*, London: Falmer Press.

Coulling, N. (2000) 'Definitions of successful education for the "looked after" child: a multi-agency perspective', *Support for Learning* 15 (1), 30–35.

Creese, A.. *et al.* (1997) *Teacher Support Teams in Primary and Secondary Schools: Resource materials for teachers*, London: David Fulton Publishers.

Croll, P. and Moses, D. (2000) *Special Needs in the Primary School: One in five?*, London: Cassell.

CSIE (Centre for Studies on Inclusive Education) (2000) *Index for Inclusion: Developing learning and participation in schools*, Bristol: CSIE.

Daniels, H. *et al.* (2000) 'Supporting collaborative problem-solving in schools', in Daniels, H. (ed.) *Special Education Re-formed: Beyond rhetoric?*, 173–186. London: Falmer Press.

Davie, R. and Galloway, D. (eds) (1996) *Listening to Children in Education*, London: David Fulton Publishers.

Denzin, N. K. (1970) *The Research Act in Sociology: A theoretical introduction to sociological method*, London: Butterworth.

Dessent, T. (1987) *Making the Ordinary School Special*, London: Falmer Press.

DfEE (Department for Education and Employment) (1997) *Excellence for All Children: Meeting special educational needs*, London: The Stationery Office.

DfEE (Department for Education and Employment), (1998a) *Meeting Special Educational Needs: A programme of action*, London: DfEE.

DfEE (Department for Education and Employment) (1998b) Circular 10/98: Section 550A of the Education Act 1996: *The Use of Force to Control or Restrain Pupils*, London:DfEE.

DfEE (Department for Education and Employment), (1998c) *Teaching: High status, high standards: Requirements for courses of initial teacher training*, Circular Number 4/98. London: DfEE.

DfEE (Department for Education and Employment), (1998d) *Supporting the Target Setting Process: Guidance for effective target setting for pupils with special educational needs*, London: DfEE.

DfEE (Department for Education and Employment) (2000a) *Promoting positive handling strategies for pupils with severe behavioural difficulties* (Draft for consultation), London:DfEE.

DfEE (Department for Education and Employment), (2000b) *SEN Code of Practice on the identification and assessment of pupils with special educational needs* (Draft for consultation), London: DfEE.

Dodd, L. and Saltmarsh, L. (2000) 'Joined-up working', *Special Children*, **127**, March, 24–27.

DOH (Department of Health) (1991*) Children in the Public Care: A review of residential child care*, London:HMSO.

DOH (Department of Health) (1993) *Guidance on Permissable Forms of Control in Children's Residential Care*, London: DOH.

Dunsmore, A. (1998) 'Improving science attainment and student self-esteem', *Improving Schools* 1 (2), 54–58.

Dwivedi, K. and Gupta, A. (2000) "Keeping cool": anger management through group work', *Support for Learning* 15 (2), 76–81.

Dyson, A. (1998) 'Professional intellectuals from powerful groups: wrong from the start?', in Clough, P. and Barton, L. (eds) *Articulating with Difficulty: Research voices in inclusive education*, 1–15. London: Paul Chapman Publishing.

Education Act (1981) London: HMSO.

Evans, P. (2000) 'Evidence-based practice: How will we know what works? An international perspective', in Daniels, H. (ed.) *Special Education Re-formed: Beyond rhetoric?*, 69–84. London: Falmer Press.

Evers, C. W. (1999) 'From foundations to coherence in educational research', in Keeves, J. P. and Lakomski, G. (eds) *Issues in Educational Research*, 264–279. Oxford:Pergamon/Elsevier Science.

Flanders, N. (1970) *Analysing Teacher Behaviour*. Reading (MA): Addison Wesley.

Flutter, J. *et al.* (1998) *Thinking about Learning; Talking about learning: A report of the effective learning project*, Cambridge: Cambridgeshire County Council/Homerton College.

Fransella, F. and Bannister, D. (1977) *A manual of the Repertory Grid Technique*, London: Academic Press.

Freeman, A. (1988) 'Who's moving the goalposts and what game are we playing anyway?', in Barton, L. (ed.), *The Politics of Special Educational Needs*, 123–145, London: The Falmer Press.

Freeman, D. (1998) *Doing Teacher Research: From inquiry to understanding*, Pacific Grove: Heinle and Heinle Publishers.

Galloway, D. *et al.* (1996) 'Maladaptive motivational style: the role of domain specific task demand in English and mathematics', *British Journal of Educational Psychology* 66, 197–207.

Gardner, H. (1993) *Frames of Mind: The theory of multiple intelligences*, London: Fontana Press.

Garner, P. and Robinson, D. (2000) 'A good read: Which SEN books do primary teachers find influential?' *British Journal of Special Education* 27 (2), 87–92.

Gray, C. (1994) *The New Social Story Book*, Arlington: Future Horizons.

Gray, J. M. *et al.* (1999) *Improving Schools: Perfomance and potential*, Buckingham: Open University Press.

Griffiths, T. (1996) 'Teachers and pupils listening to each other', in R. Davie and D. Galloway (eds) *Listening to Children in Education*, 77–89. London: David Fulton Publishers.

Halsall, R. (ed.) (1998) *Teacher Research and School Improvement: Opening doors from the inside*. Buckingam: Open University Press.

Hanks, K. (1998) 'Monitoring students' work to raise attainment and investigate the problem of underachievement', in R. Halsall (ed.) *Teacher Research and School Improvement: Opening doors from the inside*, 167–178. Buckingham: Open University Press.

Hargreaves, D. H. (1996) *Teaching as a Research-Based Profession: Possibilities and prospects*, Teacher Training Agency Annual Lecture. London: TTA.

Hart, S. (1996) *Beyond Special Needs: Enhancing children's learning through innovative thinking*, London: Paul Chapman Publishing.

Hauser, P. *et al.* (1993) 'Attention deficit – hyperactivity disorder in people with generalized resistance to thyroid hormone', *New England Journal of Medicine* 328, 997–1001.

Head, G. and O'Neill, W. (1999) 'Introducing Feuerstein's Instrumental Enrichment in a school for children with social, emotional and behavioural difficulties', *Support for Learning* 14 (3), 122–128.

Hewstone, M. (1989) *Causal Attribution: From cognitive processes to collective beliefs,* Oxford: Blackwell Publishers.

Hitchcock, G. and Hughes, D. (1995) *Research and the Teacher: A qualitative introduction to school-based research,* 2nd edn. London: Routledge.

Holland, J, (1994) 'An apparently reluctant reader', in G. H. Bell *et al.* (eds) *Action Research, Special Needs and School Development,* 113–118. London: David Fulton Publishers.

Howie, D. (1999) 'Models and morals: meanings underpinning the scientific study of special educational needs', *International Journal of Disability, Development and Education* 46 (1), 9–24.

Josselson, R. and Lieblich, A. (eds) (1993) *The Narrative Study of Lives (Vol. 1),* Newbury Park, CA: Sage.

Keeves, J. P. and McKenzie, P. A. (1999) 'Research in education: nature, needs, and priorities', in Keeves, J. P. and Lakomski, G. (eds) *Issues in Educational Research,* Oxford: Pergamon/Elsevier Science.

Kelly, G. A. (1955) *The Psychology of Personal Constructs, Volumes 1 and 2,* New York: Norton.

Kershner, R. (1999) 'The role of school-based research in helping teachers to extend their understanding of children's learning and motivation', *Journal of In-service Education* 25 (3), 423–445.

Kershner, R. (2000) 'Recognising and responding to children as individuals' in Whitebread, D. (ed.) *The Psychology of Teaching and Learning in the Primary School,* 236–255. London: RoutledgeFalmer.

Kitchin, R. (2000) 'The researched opinions on research: disabled people and disability research', *Disability and Society* 15 (1), 25–47.

Kreft, I. and de Leeuw, J. (1998) *Introducing Multilevel Modelling,* London:Sage.

Kutnick, P. and Manson, I. (2000) 'Enabling children to learn in groups', in Whitebread, D. (ed.) *The Psychology of Teaching and Learning in the Primary School,* 78–95. London: RoutledgeFalmer.

Laslett, R. (1983) *Changing Perceptions of Maladjusted Children: 1945–1981.* London: AWMC.

Lave, J. and Wenger, E. (1991) *Situated Learning: Legitimate peripheral participation,* Cambridge: Cambridge University Press.

Lewis, A. and Lindsay, G. (eds) (2000) *Researching Children's Perspectives,* 3–20. Buckingham: Open University Press.

Littleton, K. and Light, P. (eds) (1999) *Learning with Computers: Analysing productive interaction,* London: Routledge.

Lucas, D. and Thomas, G. (2000) 'Organising classrooms to promote learning for all children: two pieces of action research', in S. Clipson-Boyles (ed.) *Putting Research into Practice in Primary Teaching and Learning*, 25–36. London: David Fulton Publishers.

McDermott, R. P. (1996) 'The acquisition of a child by a learning disability', in Chaiklin, S. and Lave, J. (eds) *Understanding Practice: Perspectives on activity and context*, 269–305. Cambridge: Cambridge University Press.

McFarlane, A. (ed.) (1997) *Information Technology and Authentic Learning*, London: Routledge.

McLarty, M. and Gibson, J. W. (2000) 'Using video technology in emancipatory research', *European Journal of Special Needs Education* **13** (2), 138–148.

Mittler, P. (2000) *Working Towards Inclusive Education: Social contexts*, London: David Fulton Publishers.

Monteith, M. (ed.) (2000) *IT for Learning Enhancement*, Revised edn. Exeter: Intellect Books.

Mosley, J. (1996) *Quality Circle Time in the Primary Classroom*, Wisbech, Cambs.: LDA.

Mugny, G. and Carugati, F. (1989) *Social Representations of Intelligence*, Cambridge: Cambridge University Press.

Norwich, B. (2000) 'Inclusion in education: from concepts, values and critique to practice', in Daniels, H. (ed.) *Special Education Re-formed: Beyond rhetoric?*, 5–30. London: Falmer Press.

Oliver, M. (1992) Changing the social relations of research production, Disability, *Handicap and Society* 7 (2), 1010 –115

Oliver, M. (1997) 'Emancipatory research: Realistic goal or impossible dream?' In C. Barnes and G. Mercer (eds) *Doing Disability Research*, Leeds: The Disability Press.

Pijl, S. J. and van den Bos, K. P. (1998) 'Decision making in uncertainty', in Clark, C. *et al.* (eds.) *Theorising Special Education*, 106–115. London: Routledge.

Portwood, M. (2000) *Understanding Developmental Dyspraxia: A textbook for students and professionals*, London: David Fulton Publishers.

QCA (Qualifications and Curriculum Authority) (1999) *The National Curriculum*, London: QCA/DfEE.

Reynolds, D. *et al.* (1994) *Advances in School Effectiveness Research and Practice*, Oxford: Pergamon.

Riding, R. and Rayner, S. (1998) *Cognitive Styles and Learning Strategies*, London: David Fulton Publishers.

Robbins, B. (2000) *Inclusive Mathematics 5–11*, London: Continuum.

Robson, C. (1993) *Real World Research*, Oxford: Blackwell.

Roethlisberger, F. J. and Dickson, W. J. (1939) *Management and the Worker*, Cambridge (MA): Harvard University Press.

Rose, R. (2000) 'Using classroom support in a primary school: a single school case study', *British Journal of Special Education* 27 (4), 191–196.

Rowe, C. (1999) 'Do social stories benefit children with autism in mainstream primary schools?', *British Journal of Special Education* 26 (1), 12–14.

Rudduck, J. *et al.* (1996) *School Improvement: What can pupils tell us?*, London: David Fulton Publishers.

Rutter, M. (1989) 'Attention-deficit disorder/hyperkinetic syndrome: Conceptual and research issues regarding diagnosis and classification', in Sagvolden, T. and Archer, T. (eds), *Attention Deficit Disorder Clinical and Basic Research*, Hillsdale, N.J.:Erlbaum.

Schindele, R. A. (1985) 'Research methodology in special education: a framework approach to special problems and special solutions', in Hegarty, S. and Evans, P. (eds) *Research and Evaluation Methods in Special Education*, 3–24. Windsor: NFER-Nelson.

Sergeant, J. (ed.) (1995) *Eunythydis: European Approaches to Hyperkinetic Disorder.* Amsterdam: Sergeant.

Sherratt, D. (1999) 'Teaching children with autism to use pretend play', in Teacher Training Agency: Teacher Research Grant Projects 1998, http://www.canteach.gov.uk/info/research/grant/summaries98_99.htm

Sigafoos, J. *et al.* Elkins, J. and Kerr, M. (1993) 'Short-term conductive education: an evaluation study', *British Journal of Special Education* 20 (4), 148–151.

Simons, H. and Usher, R. (eds) (2000) *Situated Ethics in Educational Research,* London: RoutledgeFalmer.

Skidmore, D. (1999a) 'Continuities and developments in research into the education of pupils with learning difficulties', *British Journal of Educational Studies* 47 (1), 3–16.

Skidmore, D. (1999) 'Divergent discourses of learning difficulty' *British Educational Research Journal* 25 (5), 651–663.

Smeaton, R. F. (1999) *Researching Education: Reference tools and networks,* Hull: Librarians of Institutes and Schools of Education (LISE).

Sontag, J. C. (1996) 'Towards a comprehensive theoretical framework for disability research: Bronfenbrenner revisited', *Journal of Special Education* 30 (3), 319–344.

Sonuga-Barke, T. *et al.* (1992) 'Hyperactivity and delay aversion II: the effects of self versus externally imposed stimulus presentation periods on memory', *Journal of Child Psychology and Psychiatry* 33, 339–409.

Spalding, B. (2000) 'The contribution of 'Quiet Place' to early intervention strategies for children with emotional and behavioural difficulties in mainstream schools', *British Journal of Special Education* 27 (3), 129–134.

Stenhouse, L. (1983) 'Research as a basis for teaching', An inaugural lecture in the University of East Anglia, February 1979, reprinted in *Authority, Education and Emancipation,* 177–195. London: Heinemann Educational Books.

Tannock, R. (1998) 'ADHD: Advances in cognitive, neurological and genetic research', *Journal of Child Psychology and Psychiatry* **39** (1), 65–69.

Thompson. R. (1993) *The Brain: A neuroscience primer,* 2nd edn. New York: Freeman.

Tizard, B. (1991) 'Educational research and educational policy: is there a link?', *Educational and Child Psychology* **8**, 6–15.

Tobin, M. (1996) 'Optimising the use of sensory information', in N. Bozic and H. Murdoch (eds) *Learning through Interaction: Technology and children with multiple disabilities,* 56–65. London: David Fulton Publishers.

Tod, J. (2000) *IEPs – Dyslexia,* London: David Fulton Publishers.

Torrance, D. A. (2000) 'Qualitative studies into bullying within special schools', *British Journal of Special Education* **27** (1), 16–21.

TTA (1998) Teacher Training Agency Statement on Research, reproduced in *Research Intelligence,* **63**, p.16.

Urquhart, I. (2000) 'Teaching children with emotional difficulties', in Whitebread, D. (ed.) *The Psychology of Teaching and Learning in the Primary School,* 323–346. London: RoutledgeFalmer.

Vulliamy, G. and Webb, R. (eds) (1992) *Teacher Research and Special Educational Needs,* London: David Fulton Publishers.

Vygotsky, L. (1986) *Thought and Language,* revised and edited by Kozulin, A. Cambridge (MA): MIT Press.

Whitebread, D. (2000) 'Teaching children to think, reason, solve problems and be creative', in D. Whitebread, D. (ed.) *The Psychology of Teaching and Learning in the Primary School,* 140–164. London: RoutledgeFalmer.

Wolfendale, S. (ed.) (2000) *Special Needs in the Early Years: Snapshots of practice,* London: RoutledgeFalmer.

Index